PATHWAY TO CONVERSATIONAL PRAYER

*For those who talk to God but cannot
hear Him, and those who do not
know what to say.*

Okey Onuzo M.D.

To my father, Francis, and my mother, Adeline,
who established the family altar where I first learned to pray

All Biblical quotations are from the KJV unless
other-wise indicated

THIRD EDITION

Copyright © 2020 by Okey Onuzo
Published by Life Link Worldwide Inc.
175 Raymond Court, Fayetteville GA 30214 USA
ISBN: 978-1-880608-15-9
0123456789

TABLE OF CONTENTS

ACKNOWLEDGEMENTS

The inspiration to write a book like this always comes from the Lord. But most times, He uses other believers to spur us on to share this grace we carry in earthen vessels with others to reach out and bless the body of Christ universal. So all the glory must first go to the Lord our God for His enabling grace.

I must also acknowledge the great support I received for the first edition from the ladies of the Ikeja chapter of the Full Gospel Business Men's Fellowship International, here in Lagos, Nigeria. These ladies consistently pressured me to put these thoughts down on paper after sharing them at a Wednesday Prayer and Fasting meeting sometime in 1988. I cannot forget that the late Uloma Wachuku consistently urged me to produce the book at a good time for her to read.

I acknowledge the help I received from my dear friends Toyin and Femi Ogundipe: Femi for going through the manuscript carefully and pointing out several errors that needed correction. In the same vein, I must acknowledge Femi's mother, the late Mrs. Phebean Ogundipe, a renowned author of a very popular English textbook for secondary schools, who listened to me discuss the book's content in great detail. Afterward, she encouraged me to publish the book as she felt it would gain a good reception.

To a large extent, this book is a summary of several years of study and sharing with others both here in Nigeria and abroad. Therefore, I must acknowledge those many fine Christians I have had the privilege and opportunity to share with either physically or in print. Only eternity will reveal indeed how much this book is "a product of all our sermons."

In preparing this third edition, I would like to acknowledge the editorial help of Nneka Okonkwo, who went over the book to get it ready.

Finally, I wish to thank the Lord for my family, Mariam, and our four children, Dilichi, Chinaza, Dinachi, and Chibundu, who have continued to support me fully in all my endeavors.

To God be all the glory forever, Amen.

November 2020

INTRODUCTION

As a small child learning to pray at the family altar, one of the songs that impressed me most was written by James Montgomery (1771-1854):

Prayer is the soul's sincere desire,

Uttered or unexpressed,

The motions of a hidden fire

That trembles in the breast.

Prayer is the burden of a sigh,

The falling of a tear,

The upward glancing of an eye

When none but God is near.

Prayer is the simplest form of speech

That infant lips can try

Prayer the sublimest strains that reach

The majesty on high.

Prayer is the Christian's vital breath,

The Christian's native air,

His watchword at the gates of death;

He enters heaven with prayer.

O thou by whom we come to God

The life, the Truth, the way

The path of prayer Thyself hast trod

Lord teach us how to pray.

Hymn 531 from Redemption Hymnal

In my later years as a young convert to our Lord Jesus Christ, I faced the challenge of prayer. As I listened to preacher after preacher expound on the subject, I started to wonder how one can truly begin to pray.

I was taught about wrestling with God, prevailing in prayer, the struggle of prayer, the burden of prayer. I wondered how I could enter into all these diverse experiences as a prerequisite to a useful Christian life that testifies to the goodness and glory of God.

As a young convert counseling with other converts, I came across people who confessed that they could not pray. They often said that they did not know how to pray.

I recall one gentleman who always passed on prayer. The reason was that he really could not pray. At best, the impression he gave was that he couldn't sound like other people he had heard pray in public. So, he did not want to expose his ignorance publicly.

I recall on several occasions when I had had the privilege to lead a meditation on the subject of prayer: I had wondered whether I was getting across to the people.

In all my years as a believer in our Lord Jesus Christ, I found that there is something simple about prayer, as earlier expressed by the song I learned in my childhood, especially the second and third verses.

This book is not about the theology of prayer. It is not even an exposition on prayer. It is merely an attempt directed by the Holy Spirit to assist fellow pilgrims on the way to commune with our Father in heaven.

Those who have often been heard to say, "I do not know how to pray" may find this book useful. I pray that the Holy Spirit will use this work to lead men and women into the habit of daily communion with God.

CHAPTER ONE

THE NEW BIRTH AND PRAYER

DIFFICULTIES ON THE PATH

It is difficult for churchgoing people, especially those who are very religious, to appreciate the need to be born again. The reason is partly that they were brought up in a religious way of life, and they have strictly kept their religion as far as possible. There have been lapses here and there, naturally, but their religious upbringing provided them with answers that satisfied them. The somber atmosphere of worship had always provided a soothing effect and, at times, excitement. The Church programs had provided an avenue for Christian service that uplifted their souls.

I had that kind of background. There were children's services while we were young, the choir, then being an altar boy, then school. The reality of exams at school provided its pull. We prayed now and again. God answered and met our needs.

I recall, however, that God was always someone out there. He was a good God. If you prayed fervently, He always answered. But really, there was no closeness, no fondness, no musings together. I realized this lack of a personal, intimate relationship with God, but I felt it was because I had not tried hard enough. I thought it was because I had too many sinful distractions and little prayer meditation.

THE PULL

Experience has taught me that the setting of new birth for a soul is often unusual. I walked into an SU (Scripture Union) as a guest one afternoon in Enugu, Nigeria. The preacher was fiery. That's all I can remember. The details are fuzzy now, but it was all about the judgment of sinners and the grace of God. Then he came to the altar-call and prayed for those who cared to stand. As soon as the meeting was over, I got up and left.

I am sure those who invited me were thoroughly disappointed, but not for long. As I retraced my steps back home, a distance of just one or two kilometers, I suddenly became aware that I was being spoken to. It was entirely new.

Someone said to me in my heart, "Go back and write your name down. That is where you belong. You do not belong to where you are going."

It was much later that I realized that what I was going through was in accord with the word of God, where it said, "If you hear His voice, you should not harden your heart" (Psalm 95:7-8).

It is not unusual for someone not to recognize this pull. Sometimes some do recognize it and suppress it because of the pressures and demands of life.

It is not often also that the consequences, or rather the results, of responding to this pull, are well known to those who respond. Usually, the impression of the effects of responding to this pull towards God and Christ by the Holy Spirit comes from other people's prejudices, from people who may be downright rebels, dropouts, or antagonists.

To someone responding to an altar call, Christianity is often a fuzzy thing, depending of course, on his or her religious background. If one's experience were Church based religion, the question would likely be, "What is new?" If the background was not very religious or religious, but of a different persuasion, the question would probably be: What is this whole thing about?

THE NEW BIRTH

Answering an altar call is like going through a birth process. An individual senses the pull towards God by the Spirit of God. He kneels in prayer in recognition of his guilt as a sinner. He seeks cleansing from the atoning blood of Jesus. He accepts Jesus as Lord over his life and subsequently rises from his prayers, a new creature. But the question often asked is, how new?

Many people have testified that they never felt any different after that sort of experience. Some have even claimed that they have never felt anything different at any time.

The secret to the chemistry of the new birth hinges on two keywords: Sincerity and Decision.

The first question to be settled is, "Was that repentance sincere? Was there revulsion at a life of total sinfulness? That is, doing your own thing, your own way, just like everybody else, or was it an emotionally charged confession that is often related to a particular experience and did not address the very question of a habitual life of sin?"

The next question to be settled is, "Was it a decision to follow Christ?" We all know what a decision is. Decisions are dynamic by their very nature. They must bring about change. If a person indeed decides to follow Christ, the one result of such a decision is a sincere driving desire to discover what following Christ involves. If this basic desire is not there, it is difficult to say that there had been a genuine decision.

THE NEW BIRTH AND THE RELATIONSHIP

The new birth or being born again is not a gateway to a new religion. If anything, the new birth is a departure from an often sterile religious way of life to a dynamic relationship.

The difference between religion and relationship in Christianity is that religion is a measure of one's observance of a set of rules and regulations. A relationship, on the other hand, has a beginning. One day it was not there; then, another day, it had begun.

Again, a relationship is warm and natural. It grows with more understanding. The degree of intimacy grows with greater understanding.

Some people may go through a new birth experience and come out religious again without the relationship.

We would refer to their experience as a spiritual stillbirth. The implication is that the person did go through a spiritual birth process but did not come alive at the end of it.

THE SPIRITUAL MECHANICS OF THE NEW BIRTH

It might be helpful to try to explain what happens when a person is born again so that one can judge his or her experience.

We may recall that our Lord Jesus Christ first mentioned this idea of being born again in His discussions with Nicodemus in the Gospel of John, chapter 3:1-7.

I believe it is in verse 6 that we get the true meaning of the whole concept. Our Lord Jesus declared: "That which is born of the flesh is flesh, and that which is born of the Spirit is spirit."

The implication of this is that every man is supposed to have two kinds of birth. The first is natural birth or biological birth. I am sure that it needs no explanation. But it is important to note, though, that natural birth is also a process. At the end of the process, a baby may be born alive or born dead, i.e., a stillbirth.

Spiritual birth, on the other hand, bears some explanation. To appreciate it, we must go back a little to man's nature and explore it thoroughly so that the mechanics of spiritual birth will have some meaning.

THE TRIPARTITE NATURE OF MAN

The Bible teaches us that a man has three parts to him. The first part is the body, which we are told was formed from the dust of the earth (Genesis.2:7). Anybody familiar with introductory biology can appreciate that readily. The human anatomy is part and parcel of matter. Indeed, we are part of the elements. So the nature of our bodies is not in doubt at all.

The Bible goes further to say, in the same Genesis 2:7, that after the human biology was in place, the LORD God Almighty proceeded to impart His nature into this His lifeless creation.

In the creation of man, therefore, we recognize a sequence. First was the body from the dust of the earth. Next, the Spirit of God entered into the body. When the Spirit of God made contact with this body, human consciousness, otherwise known as the soul, was born. So we see that the body is integral and a part of the matter. The spirit is also integral and a part of God. Human consciousness or the soul, on the other hand, is the by-product of the contact between the Spirit of God and matter.

The creative process outlined above is the origin of the tripartite or the three natures of man: the body, the soul, and the spirit.

It is essential to understand this basic composition of man. It is very relevant to the relationship between God and man.

This tripartite nature may explain why some draw three concentric circles to represent the nature of man. The body is the outermost, and the spirit is the innermost; in between them is the soul.

THE THREE NATURES OF MAN AND THE FALL

Some people misunderstand the story of the fall of man as recorded in Genesis 3. Some of the reasons adduced for the fall range from the absurd to the ludicrous. I have heard people say that it was due to sexual immorality or some legendary poisonous fruit.

When we examine the story in some detail as recorded in Genesis 3:1-24, we are made to face God's idea of how He wants His world organized. What we learn is that there were two unique trees in the Garden of Eden. The first was the *tree of the knowledge of good and evil*. The second was the *tree of life*. Let us examine these two trees more closely.

TREE OF KNOWLEDGE OF GOOD AND EVIL

For us to be able to appreciate the place of this tree in God's idea of running His world, I believe we should stop to ask ourselves whether Adam and Eve had any knowledge of good and evil before they ate the fruit from that tree. I think the obvious answer is yes. Adam and Eve knew good from evil or right from wrong before they ate the forbidden fruit. The only difference was that their knowledge of good and evil derived entirely from God. In other words, if God said A was good, then A was good. If God said B was bad, then B was bad. God was their reference point for determining good and evil. How do I know this, you may ask?

Let us read the devil's statement in Genesis 3:4-5:

And the Serpent said Ye shall not surely die.

For God doth know that in the day you eat thereof, then your eyes shall be opened, and ye shall be as gods, knowing good and evil.
--Genesis 3:4-5

This trick suggestion was a coup par excellence. The devil was encouraging Adam and Eve to rebel from God's control.

Hitherto they had accepted God's control volitionally. But the devil was saying to them: "If you were to take that fruit, you would be on your own. You would not need God anymore to tell you what is good and what is evil."

THE TREE OF LIFE

On the other hand, the tree of life symbolized God's reward for consistent compliance with His commandments. The letter sent to the Church at Ephesus by our Lord Jesus Christ, through the revelations He granted John, the apostle, established this.

He that hath an ear let him hear what the Spirit saith unto the churches; To him that overcometh will I give to eat of the *tree of life*, which is in the midst of the paradise of God.
—Revelation 2:7

For Adam and Eve, what would have qualified them in due course to partake of the fruit of the *tree of life*, was a consistent avoidance of the *tree of knowledge of good and evil*. What this would have meant was that they would have remained permanently under God's control.

God expected them to have consistently resisted the temptation of the devil to rebel from His control. That explains why the tree of life was within their reach in the Garden of Eden in Genesis 3:22-24.

"And the LORD God said. Behold, the man is become as one of us, to know good and evil: and now, lest he put forth his hand, and also take of the tree of life, and eat, and live forever: Therefore the LORD God sent him forth from the Garden of Eden, to till the ground from whence he was taken. So He drove out the man; and He placed at the east of the garden of Eden Cherubims and a flaming sword which turned every way, to keep the way of the tree of life."

Immortality in the flesh was within reach of humanity but for the tragedy of eating the forbidden fruit. By eating fruit from the *tree of knowledge of good and evil,* Adam and Eve robbed themselves and all humanity with them of the opportunity of immortality in the flesh. Had they remained faithful to the LORD God Almighty, death would have been unknown in human experience.

SOUL VERSUS SPIRIT CONTROL

When God determined good and evil for Adam and Eve, He was in control of their lives. This control is what we know in the New Testament as being led by the Spirit of God. The Spirit of God in man, imparted into the man at creation, was the source of his insight into what was right and what was wrong. The part of the Spirit of God deposited in man became the human spirit. Before the fall, the human spirit was in constant and direct communion with the Spirit of God. This linkage served to reveal God's will to the man in any and every situation so that he would obey it without question.

But when man ate the forbidden fruit, he automatically disabled the linkage between the Spirit of God and the human spirit and dethroned and displaced the duo from the control center of his life. He took over the controls himself. In other words, human consciousness called the soul replaced the spirit in man as the center of man's life.

Unfortunately, eating the forbidden fruit had violated the law of life in the Garden of Eden stated in **Genesis 2:16-17 (NKJV)**

16 And the LORD God commanded the man, saying, "Of every tree of the garden you may freely eat;

17 but of the tree of the knowledge of good and evil you shall not eat, for in the day that you eat of it you shall surely die."

It is an open question whether the man understood the commandment. Notwithstanding, death followed the eating of the forbidden fruit. It was not physical death but spiritual death, which is the permanent disconnection of that crucial linkage between the human spirit and the Spirit of God. Without the Spirit of God's dominant input, man's spirit came under the human will and competed with the man's thoughts and feelings to control the will and its decisions. For this reason, many would say that the conscience of man resides in the human spirit. There, it serves to alert us when we are about to go in the wrong direction in life.

The soul consists of three main parts: the will, the intellect, and the emotions or feelings. This distinction is why we now can describe a person as being willful or intellectual or logical or just emotional. What this means is that the predominant influence in his conduct is either his strong will or lack of it, or his healthy intellectual and logical mind or lack of it, or his or her overbearing emotional response or lack of it.

Let us therefore understand and appreciate that all these are by-products of the fall of man. It was not so at the beginning in the Garden of Eden.

THE DEATH OF SPIRIT CONTROL

The spirit in man was imparted into him by God at creation. So each new creation receives the same quantum of the Spirit of God.

Before Adam and Eve ate the forbidden fruit, the Spirit of God always told them what to do by communicating the mind of God to them via their human spirit, which initially came from God. At that stage, man was God-centered in his life. His spirit, which was alive and vibrant, formed the link between him and God.

But after he ate the forbidden fruit, the spirit in man was de-linked from the Spirit of God and so lost the control of man's life to his soul. This de-linking is why the spirit in man after the fall is said to be dead. This death is spiritual because the Spirit of God broke the link with the spirit in man. Thus the spirit of all the offspring of Adam, which includes you and me, is dead.

When David said in Psalm 51:5: "In sin did my mother conceive me," he was speaking of this stigma of rebellion that had become an intrinsic part of all the offspring of Adam. All humanity is born in sin. The spirit is not in control of life. The soul cannot make the right choices consistently. Here is the summary of this state of affairs in **Genesis 6:5-6 (NKJV)**

5 Then the LORD saw that the wickedness of man *was* great in the earth, and *that* every intent of the thoughts of his heart *was* only evil continually. 6 And the LORD was sorry that He had made man on the earth, and He was grieved in His heart.

When the man was left to make the choice he opted for by eating the forbidden fruit, it became evident that his natural tendency was to do evil or wrong rather than right.

Philosophers over the ages, as they searched for the route to man's escape from his cycle of death and destruction, erred when they called on us all to take our destinies into our own hands and rediscover the innate powers we have within us to redeem ourselves.

As we can see, this sort of call is a further departure from the state of affairs at the Garden of Eden before the fall.

THE NEW BIRTH REVISITED

With this background in our minds, let us proceed to examine the concept of new birth again to appreciate what Jesus was saying. In John 3:3: Jesus did say to Nicodemus, "Ye must be born again."

In verse 6, He said, "You have been born by the flesh; you now need to be born by the spirit."

In John 1:12-13, the Bible says:

But as many as received Him, to them gave He power to become the sons of God, even to them that believe on His name: Which were born, not of blood, nor of the will of the flesh, nor of the will of man, but of God.

It is evident from all these that with the coming of our dear Lord and Saviour Jesus Christ into the world, God established a process for the correction of this spiritual death that took place in the Garden of Eden.

It would also appear that those who went through the spiritual birth process of accepting Jesus Christ as Lord had the privilege of the LORD God Almighty re-establishing the connection between their human spirit and the Spirit of God. It is this reconnection that gives their spirit the potential to dominate and control their soul once again. This reconnection is what it means to be born again or to be born of the Spirit of God.

However, we must note that the absolute path to deciding what a man does in his life still rests with his will. But the quickened human spirit under pressure and influence from the Spirit of God can now bring the mind of God to bear on the thoughts and feelings to bend the will. When the man, exercising free choice, decides to obey the Spirit of God, the soul is said to be dethroned again, while the spirit is said to have regained control.

I believe this is why many people claim they never felt any different on the day of their new birth, but subsequently, they became aware that something had happened to them. Some don't feel it immediately because it is a 'spiritual surgery,' not a physical one. You dethrone one "man" from the control and enthrone another. Subsequently, as the new control arrangement begins to function, the effect starts to be felt, and so they become aware that something definite had happened to them. Some people do sense it immediately, though. For others, it takes a little while to come.

But some people still say that nothing did happen after that. In light of our ongoing discussion, it is easy to see why no change emerged in the end. The most obvious reason is that although the individual may have gone through a birth process, the procedure did not lead to a switch of controls from soul to spirit.

They would always notice the switch, for once the controls are changed, the individual moves away from self-centredness to God-centredness. There will exist a hunger to know and do what pleases God according to the Bible.

It is essential to mention that although we are born again and have become children of God by adoption (Romans 8:16 and Ephesians 1:5), the Spirit's control of every area of our lives is never fully completed until we appear before Christ; for the Bible declares that when we see Him in His glory, the vestiges or pockets of the rebellion left in some areas of our lives will clear immediately, as we bow in total final surrender (1 John 3:2)

THE NEW BIRTH AND THE RELATIONSHIP

In concluding this discourse on the new birth, it is important to recap the vital relationship between being born again and developing a relationship with God.

Let me state very categorically that there can be no genuine experience of the new birth without the onset of a vibrant relationship with God. This relationship is the crux of the matter and is very important.

Before our Lord Jesus came, men had their religions. After He came, He ushered in a relationship. It is through this relationship that a deep communion between the human spirit and the Spirit of the living God is re-established. The Spirit of the living God that decodes God's mind transmits the message from God to man through the spirit in man. On the other hand, the spirit in the man who knows man's mind transmits man's thoughts and feelings to God through the Spirit of God.

But as it is written eyes hath not seen, nor ears heard, neither have entered the heart of man, the things which God hath prepared for them that love Him. But God hath revealed them unto us by His Spirit: for the spirit searcheth all things, yea the deep things of God. For what man knoweth the things of a man, save the spirit of man which is in him?" Even so the things of God knoweth no man, but the Spirit of God. Now we have received (at our new birth) not the spirit of the world, but the spirit which is of God; that we might know the things which are freely given to us of God.

—1 Corinthians 2:9-12

It is this cross-fertilization that is the hub of the new relationship ushered in at the new birth. It is a new perception of the presence of

God that blossoms with an obedient response to the promptings of the Spirit of God communicated to us through our spirit.

Therefore, it is very easy to see that the new birth is not a call to another religion. Religion, by its nature, is ritualistic and very often dead. Religion is a result of man's imagination: what usually happens is that man devises ways of reaching God and begins a series of rituals to establish it.

The true worship of God is spiritual. The human spirit must come alive. By that, I mean that the human spirit must resume the control of man's life if he is to worship God in spirit and in truth. Our Lord Jesus Christ said:

But the hour cometh, and now is, when the true worshipers shall worship the Father in spirit and in truth: for the Father seeketh such to worship Him.

God is a spirit, and they that worship Him, must worship Him in spirit and in truth.

—John 4:23-24

CHAPTER TWO

THE NEW RELATIONSHIP

THE BEGINNING

The beginning of any new relationship is usually marked by some degree of reservation, if not suspicion. There is always this feeling of uncertainty about going forward because one may not have the disposition to continue.

For some people, it may be the reverse. They may have embraced a new relationship with profuse enthusiasm only to discover that there are issues that dampen the spirit. Our Lord Jesus painted this picture in the parable of the sower (Mark 4:4-9).

Whatever the initial reaction, the fact remains that a new relationship is usually approached with a reasonable degree of caution until the parties get to know each other better. That at least should be the sensible attitude to a new relationship, if for no other reason, at least as protection against surprises and disappointments.

The other thing about a new relationship is that it thrives on knowledge. There would be no meaningful relationship unless the parties involved got to know each other.

I recall my beginnings in 1970. I doubt that I had much clue of what Christianity was all about. I simply responded to an altar call. But after that response, I recall that I had viewed the whole thing with great reservation, if not outright suspicion. I was undoubtedly skeptical about some of the rather austere and ascetic practices I observed among other brethren around and wondered if I could ever be or look like them.

It was popular in those days to call on the brethren to ensure that they had made a total commitment of their lives to God in Christ Jesus. That was a call I viewed with tremendous suspicion because I figured that would mean I wouldn't be able to make my decisions myself. I found that notion very unacceptable at the time and was determined not to say any such prayer. Besides, I had secret ambitions I had nursed for ages, and I never wanted anything or anyone to tamper with them.

I did hold out for one long year until I was stimulated by one preacher to rethink my position. The way he put it satisfied me and enabled me to surrender. His point was that: One can never be better than God can make him.

In other words, if you had a secret ambition, you do not have to be afraid that God would alter it all even though He might sometimes. But you must believe that even in realizing that ambition, God can get you to your destination faster and easier than you could ever get yourself. That appealed to me greatly, and I let go.

Much later, I got to know that He does alter ambitions now and again when He sees that we are heading in the wrong direction. But I was glad the preacher didn't get to that level on that day. I was ready for lesson one only, not lesson four.

This kind of reservation often marks the beginning of any relationship. Sometimes the reservation is so severe that there is practically no spiritual progress. By that, I mean no real progress in the area of the Spirit control of the lives hitherto dominated by the soul represented by the will, the emotion, or the intellect. Some only seek the Spirit's direction and control occasionally or whenever there is a problem. But so long as things appear to be going well, it would be business as usual. They make their decisions based on the way they feel, think, or will. There is no concerted effort to consistently discern the voice of the Spirit of God in their lives.

But where does the control center reside? Is it in the soul or the spirit? This is the question at this very early stage of the spiritual journey. Sometimes the spirit is called in for advice. At other times he is sent away on vacation, as it were.

The beginning of the new birth relationship should leave us in no doubt about who is in charge. The spirit is in charge. The soul must bow to the spirit control, for it is the spirit that is in touch with the Spirit of God and can reveal God's will. The Spirit of God knows God's will.

But this may sound all so abstract or metaphysical. Many will naturally wonder, "Where is the spirit, and where is the soul? Are they both not the same?"

The reason for this seeming confusion is not difficult to find. Before the new birth the spirit was dead. So the soul was everything. After the new birth, the spirit came back alive, but the soul is still looming large.

The Bible reveals a way to begin to separate them until the spirit is freed from the constraints of the soul and body.

For the word of God is quick, and powerful and sharper than any two-edged sword, piercing even to the dividing asunder of soul and spirit, and of the joints and marrow, and is a discerner of the thoughts and intents of the heart.

—Hebrews 4:12

The Bible says here that when a man reads and understands God's word, God's thoughts become like a cleavage knife separating the thoughts of the world and thoughts of the man. The more he reads the Bible, the more he is familiar with God's thoughts and values. Through much study, this mind renewal process progresses until he can differentiate God's mind from his personal opinion and the opinions of men.

With progression, his thoughts that originate from his environment, the input of his desires, and the world's pressured opinions can all be teased apart so that he can discern in which direction the Spirit of God is leading.

I believe this is why individuals differ in their ability to sense their spirits' communication. If they read, believe, and obey God's word, then cleavage progressively occurs until they can sense God readily and easily.

So the word of God in the Bible is, therefore, the cleavage knife. Those who do not read it at all will have difficulties hearing God. Those who read it but do not believe and obey it will have the same difficulties knowing when the Spirit of the Lord is speaking to their spirit.

One reason for this is that what the Spirit of God says to man's spirit cannot contradict what the Spirit of God has caused to be written down in the Bible. That bears repeating.

All Scripture is given by inspiration of God, and is profitable for doctrine, for reproof, for correction, for instruction in righteousness.

—2 Timothy 3:16

For the prophecy came not in old time by the will of man: but Holy men of God spake as they were moved by the Holy Ghost.

—2 Peter 1:21

By using what is in the Bible as the reference, man's soul is made familiar with God's thoughts. This language familiarity facilitates spiritual communication. It is a normal process of learning.

Again the words of the Bible do not only train the soul on God's thought content; it also trains it on the issue of God's manner of speech. God speaks in a certain way to people. His communication method to a particular individual is, in no small way, tailor-made and guided by the degree of intimacy that co-exists and the nature of God as revealed in the Bible.

Also, the preferred periods of communication differ. Examples abound of men like our Lord Jesus Christ, who rose a great while before dawn to commune with God (Mark 1:35). Others, like Joseph, the husband of Mary, received communication in the vision of the night (Matthew 1:20).

SENSING THE SPIRIT OF GOD—THE LEARNING PROCESS

Let us stop to address this subject very clearly. I dare to say that a victorious Christian life hinges squarely on it. One preacher did say that if we were to follow God's word closely, we would be asking Him to forgive us for some of the good things we did that were not directed by His Spirit, i.e., the good things we did in our flesh. This thought is discernible in the meaning of Romans 8:8, where it says: "So then they that are in the flesh cannot please God."

There is a story in the Bible that I find very useful when explaining this question of being able to sense the Spirit of God. Let us read along:

And the child Samuel ministered unto the Lord before Eli. And the word of the Lord was precious in those days; there was no open vision.

And it came to pass at that time when Eli was laid down in his place, and his eyes began to wax dim, that he could not see;

And ere the lamp of God went out in the temple of the Lord, Where the ark of God was, and Samuel was laid down to sleep;

That the Lord called Samuel: and he answered. Here am I.

And he ran unto Eli, and said, Here am I; for thou calledst me. And he said, I called not; lie down again.

And he went and lay down.

And the Lord called yet again, Samuel, And Samuel arose and went to Eli, and said, Here am I; for thou didst call me. And he answered I called not, my son, lie down again.

Now Samuel did not yet know the Lord; neither was the word of the Lord yet revealed unto him.

And the Lord called Samuel again the third time. And he arose and went to Eli, and said, Here am I; for thou didst call me. And Eli perceived that the Lord had called the child.

Therefore Eli said unto Samuel, Go lie down: and it shall be if he calls thee, that thou shalt say, Speak, Lord; for thy servant heareth. So Samuel went and lay down in his place.

And the Lord came, and stood, and called as at other times, Samuel, Samuel. Then Samuel answered, Speak; for thy servant heareth.

—1 Samuel 3:1-10

I find this a fascinating story with respect to this study on sensing the Spirit of God.

Samuel was very young. But being young had nothing to do with it. The crucial fact revealed in this story is actually in verse seven, which says: "Now Samuel did not yet know the Lord neither was the word of the Lord yet revealed unto him."

In other words, at that stage of Samuel's relationship with God, he could not sense God. The word of the Lord was yet to be revealed unto him. That means the cleavage between his soul and his spirit had not even begun. The training of his soul using God's word had not begun.

Under the circumstances, Samuel had to depend on someone else's guidance to sense God.

This dependence is not too uncommon an experience in Christian circles. Some people move from fellowship to fellowship and from preacher to preacher, seeking to know the mind of God about one thing in their lives or the other.

Sometimes this is no more than spiritual laziness, or more appropriately, a human penchant for short-cuts. They cannot submit themselves to the word of God to achieve this cleavage between their soul and their Spirit so that their human spirit can freely sense the Spirit of God and transmit the information to a prepared and functioning receptor, the soul. They would rather have someone else do it for them and tell them whatever God is saying.

In the Old Testament dispensation, that would be acceptable because that was the way things were. The prophets and the priests and occasionally, the king-prophets only had and could sense the mind of God.

But in this New Testament setting, after God had freely poured His Holy Spirit upon all flesh, beginning at Pentecost, that position has become altogether untenable. Potentially, therefore, every Christian, and by that, I mean every born-again Christian, can sense the Spirit of God and thereby function in the same way as an Old Testament prophet. But let us return to Samuel and his learning process. Eli, the prophet-judge, taught Samuel to respond to God in the same way as he, Samuel, answered him. It was Samuel's baptism or initiation if you prefer it.

Subsequently, we find that Samuel had come a long, long way from this initiation. Unfortunately, we hear about this again when Samuel was old, in 1 Samuel 8:7 and 16:1-13.

"And Samuel prayed unto the Lord,

'And the Lord said unto Samuel, Hearken unto the voice of the people in all that they say unto thee: for they have not rejected thee, but they have rejected Me, that I should not reign over them.'" (1 Samuel 8:7)

This Scripture is a dialogue between God and Samuel on the matter of the people's decision to switch from direct theocracy to representative theocracy by opting to have a king in Israel. Samuel prayed to the Lord about the issue on hand. God told him exactly what to do. Give the children of Israel the king they want. It's Me they have rejected, not you.

But there is even a more classic example when Samuel chose David as the second king of Israel after Saul. The very first verse of 1 Samuel, chapter 16, reads: "And the Lord said unto Samuel, How long wilt thou mourn for Saul, seeing I have rejected him from reigning over Israel. Fill thine horn with oil, and go, I will send thee to Jesse the Beth-le-hemite, for I have provided Me a king among his sons."

What has transpired here is communication. God sensed the sorrow in Samuel's heart and told him what to do to solve the problem.

But in David's choice as king from among his brothers, we see the communication exchanges between the soul and the spirit. The apostle Paul summarized it classically in 2 Corinthians 5:7 when he said: "For we walk by faith [the spirit sensor] not by sight [one of the soul's sensors]."

Let's pick up the story from 1 Samuel 16:6.

"And it came to pass, when they were come, that he looked on Eliab, and said, [to God obviously] 'surely the Lord's anointed is before him.'

But the Lord said unto Samuel, 'look not on his countenance, or on the height of his stature; because I have refused him: for the Lord seeth not as man seeth: for man looketh on the outward appearance, but the Lord looketh on the heart.'

Then Jesse called Abinadab and made him pass before Samuel, and he [Samuel] said, 'Neither hath the Lord chosen this.'

Then Jesse made Shammah to pass by. And he [Samuel] said, 'Neither hath the Lord chosen this.'

Again, Jesse made seven of his sons to pass before Samuel. And Samuel said unto Jesse, 'The Lord hath not chosen these.'

And Samuel said unto Jesse, 'Are here all thy children?' And he said, 'There remaineth yet the youngest, and, behold, he keepeth the sheep.' And Samuel said unto Jesse, 'Send and fetch him: for we will not sit down till he comes hither.'

And he sent and brought him in. Now he was ruddy and withal of a beautiful countenance, and goodly to look to. And the Lord said, 'Arise, anoint him: for this is he.'

Then Samuel took the horn of oil and anointed him in the midst of his brethren: and the Spirit of the Lord came upon David from that day forward.'"

—1 Samuel 16:6-13

This account is fascinating in many respects. When Samuel arrived at Jesse's home, he had prior knowledge that a king must emerge from there. That was the definite communication from God. 1 Samuel Chapter 16:1 says: "... for I have provided me a king among his sons." But who this king was among Jesse's eight sons, he had no clue.

The moment he set eyes on Eliab and savored his kingly stature and looks, he was noticeably impressed and mused heavenwards to God, "Surely the Lord's anointed [meaning the king to be] is before him."

Samuel based his choice of Eliab only on his looks and stature: "That man looks kingly," he must have thought. "Lord," he said, "I am sure that is Your king coming."

We might say at that moment that Samuel was leaning towards Eliab. We could call this a classic example of soul judgment, based on what we see, what we hear, what we feel, et cetera.

But Samuel had his soul and his spirit cleaved apart. Despite his thoughts and feelings, therefore, he was still able to hear God well. The Spirit of God communicated God's mind on the subject in question, through his human spirit, to the mind component of his soul (the soul of man consists of the will, intellect/mind, and emotion). The LORD God delivered a mild rebuke on the dangers of "soul judgment" when He said in Verse 7: "For the Lord seeth not as man seeth, for man looketh on the outward appearance, but the Lord looketh on the heart."

Samuel took the gentle rebuke kindly and, after that, only told Jesse what the Lord had said: "The Lord has not chosen this," nor this, nor this, on and on until all the seven sons present had come and gone.

But a king must come out of this family. So Samuel insisted: "Since the Lord has not chosen any of these, there must be still someone else to come."

This kind of confidence is a beautiful thing about hearing from God. It imparts certainty to our missions when we have unambiguous instructions.

When David appeared, the Lord then said to Samuel, "Arise, anoint him, for this is he."

It was the climax of a mission, an exercise in communion, a demonstration of divine guidance, and the value of sensing the Spirit of God in our day-to-day living.

But we see that Samuel had come a long, long way from his beginnings. Initially, he could not sense God. But over the years, as Samuel walked with Almighty God in obedience, he experienced a more functional cleavage between his soul and spirit. He could tell when God was speaking. He could also tell when what he was hearing came from his thoughts or his mind.

HOW CAN I TELL WHO IS SPEAKING IN MY HEART?

I believe we need to explore this question in greater detail to attempt to solve the attendant problems of learning to sense the Spirit of God.

It is essential to bear in mind that there are three voices in the heart of each person:

The voice of God, i.e., the communion of the Spirit of God to the spirit of man: The voice of man, i.e., the total input from his soul's ruminations or the summary of the input of his senses or his will, his intellect, and his emotions: The voice of the devil, i.e., the communion of the spirit of evil to the spirit of man.

It is also important to note that these three sources are processed through the common pathway of the mind and the will, to get a man to respond. In other words, what a man does or does not do may be in response to God, himself, or the devil.

Learning to sense the Spirit of God, therefore, involves learning to distinguish the voices.

I have stated earlier that the human mind undergoes training in sensing the Spirit of God's communications to his spirit, as the individual consciously obeys God's word.

But there are areas of life that the mind of God as revealed in His word, has not explicitly addressed. Let us take an everyday example.

Suppose a friend calls to ask you to escort him on a short two-hour trip to a nearby city. Suppose also you can afford the time in your judgment. Suppose again that there is no reasonable objection to your going with him as far as you can see or imagine. But the question remains, should you go with him or should you not?

What should determine what you do as a child of God, would be what you sense the Spirit of God to be saying on the question. That communication should come to you instantly since you need the answer urgently, like Samuel, in the house of Jesse. That communication should also be clear and should be distinct from your rational analysis of the situation. If we hear what the LORD is saying clearly, then it would mean that we have a sufficient cleavage between the soul and the spirit in us.

Again, you should still sense that communication, whether it runs contrary to your judgment or in line with it.

To many people, this is the real crux of the matter. How can one tell when God is speaking?

The keyword, I believe, is learning. There was a time the prophet Samuel could not tell when God was speaking or when he or another like Judge Eli was talking. The apostle Paul addressed this issue beautifully in his first letter to the Corinthians 7:6,10,12,25.

But I speak this by permission, and not of commandment.

And unto the married I command, yet not I but the Lord--

But to the rest speak I, not the Lord--

Now concerning virgins, I have no commandment of the Lord: yet I give my judgment as one that hath obtained mercy of the Lord to be faithful.

THE LEARNING PROCESS

If we look closely at Samuel's learning process, we would immediately see that it was initially a matter of trial and error. He answered the wrong person three times. The fourth time Judge Eli initiated him into the experience of hearing from God.

Learning to sense the Spirit of God is a matter of growing in faith. Faith will bring the experience that will lead to as near certainty of what we perceive as ever can be. That is why the Apostle Paul declares unequivocally in 2 Corinthians 5:7, "For we walk by faith not by sight."

FAITH IS THE SENSOR OF THE SPIRIT

It is faith sensing that will bring the relevant experience.

A preacher suggested a way out of the dilemma, which I have found useful in sharing this thought. At the initial stages of learning to hear from God, it would seem appropriate to make a definite request like this to the Lord:

"Lord, I desire to do Your will. The only problem I have is that I do not know what You will have me do exactly. Lord, since there are three possible voices in my heart, I would like You to be the first to speak in my heart each time after I pray. LORD, this is because I will go ahead and do the first thing I hear, believing You were the One saying it."

Notice that this is where faith in God comes in. I believe that God is altogether good. If a person says a prayer like this in all sincerity, the Spirit of God will come in and aid him or her to follow God closely.

Remember that this prayer is only necessary for the so-called grey areas of life where we have no definite command in God's word. Wherever there is well-articulated teaching in the Bible on a matter, then God's mind is revealed already.

But someone may argue that this does not necessarily mean that what you hear each time is from the Lord. That is quite true. It is possible in the learning process that you may still miss what the Lord is saying to you. I dare say that the degree of correctness each time improves daily with perseverance, but I doubt that it can ever be 100 percent for anyone all the time. In other words, all of us still make mistakes here and there, now and again.

But there is a safeguard. Once a person is sincere and honestly desires to follow the Lord's leading in all things, he or she may say a second prayer that is equally important.

"Lord, if I missed what You said and I am doing the wrong thing, please stop me, and I will stop. No matter how far I have gone, I will stop once it is clear to me that stopping is what You desire."

Those who have achieved a reasonable degree of cleavage between their souls and their spirit by obeying God's word may not find this first voice choice lesson necessary. They would have accumulated experience talking and hearing from God through the Bible and dialogue.

This attitude of desiring God's will and striving to sense it each time is the bedrock of intimacy with the Lord.

As we shall see, intimacy with the Lord is the basis of effective prayer. Sensing the mind of God builds intimacy with God daily. It progressively approximates our will to the will of God until 90–100 percent of our daily actions become congruent with His desires.

This seeking of God's will in everything is not a path for the cowardly or for the doubtful. It is a path for men and women of faith.

Some keep lamenting that one cannot be very sure that God spoke to him or her. I have always felt that a mother who does not want his child to fall may never see the child walk. This lesson from life tells us that those who are learning to walk will occasionally trip and fall.

There is no doubt that there will be mistakes. But they should be honest mistakes if we are truly sincere. And God, who is seeing our desire and our struggle, will open up our channel of communication with Him until it flows naturally.

For those who are sincere, the experience they garner will soon build confidence. As confidence grows through experience, we learn to trust our communication from the Spirit of God to our spirit and so progressively base our decisions in life on those communications.

For those who can sense the voice of the Spirit of God to their spirit readily, making decisions is often an easy matter. Note that whether a case before them is weighty or complicated, they will still be able to make their decision readily and easily because they can sense the direction the Spirit of God is leading. This ease of making tough and complicated decisions reveals the power of divine omniscience and the privilege of being led by God, who knows all things.

SHARPENING OUR SPIRITUAL SENSIBILITY

Being able to sense the Spirit of God may also be enhanced by praying in other tongues.

As a young convert to our Lord Jesus Christ, I had disagreed with those who had contended quite passionately that one needed to be filled with the Holy Ghost as a post-conversion, post-water baptism experience. I had argued creditably, or so I had thought, that since it is the Holy Ghost that brings the individual to conversion, there was no need to seek another in-filling or baptism because the Holy Ghost was already in the person.

All along, I had defended this position as a carry-over from the fellowship I attended. I had never actually sat down to study the Scriptures on the subject to see whether my view was defensible.

But one day, I sat down and studied the relevant Scriptures and was most pleasantly surprised by the outcome. The Scriptures are quite clear on the matter, and there are justifiable reasons to believe that one needs to speak in tongues when he or she is baptized in the Holy Ghost.

The most convincing passage was Acts 19:1-7, where the apostle Paul pointedly asked supposed disciples whether they had received the Holy Ghost since they believed. When the people confirmed that they had never heard of the Holy Ghost, and that their revelation of God was limited to repentance and water baptism as taught by John the Baptist, the apostle took time to instruct them more accurately. He pointed out to them that John's ministry was well accommodated within the works and teachings of our Lord Jesus Christ, the only begotten Son of God.

Now let us read on from Acts 19:5:

"When they heard this, they were baptized in the name of the Lord Jesus."

By this very act, they had become born-again Christians because they had acknowledged the work of grace and salvation in Christ. Therefore, ostensibly, they were in touch with the Holy Ghost, who had drawn them to Christ. They had become believers.

But let us read on.

"And when Paul had laid his hands upon them, the Holy Ghost came on them, and they spake with tongues and prophesied" (Acts 19:6).

Disciples in Ephesus who had believed and were baptized needed the Holy Ghost to come on them after their conversion and water baptism. The same was true of the believers in Samaria in Acts 8, where it says:

Now when the apostles which were at Jerusalem heard that Samaria had received the word of God, they sent unto them Peter and John:

Who, when they were come down, prayed for them that they might receive the Holy Ghost: (For as yet He was fallen upon none of them: only they were baptized in the name of the Lord Jesus.)

Then laid they their hands on them, and they received the Holy Ghost.

—Acts 8:14-17

Earlier on in verse 12 of the same chapter, we are told,

"But when they believed Philip preaching the things concerning the kingdom of God, and the name of Jesus Christ, they were baptized both men and women."

These two passages reveal that those who believed and were baptized, needed to be filled with the Holy Ghost.

The question then is: "If they needed to be filled with the Holy Ghost, then after conversion and water baptism, why not now?"

It is difficult to find support in the Bible for the often-expressed opinion that such experiences were only necessary for that period because the Church was so young and needed all that support.

Such a position is not defensible from Scripture; not in the face of Peter's declaration in Acts 2:38-39:

"Then Peter said unto them, Repent and be baptized every one of you in the name of Jesus Christ for the remission of sins, and ye shall receive the gift of the Holy Ghost

"For the promise is unto you, and to your children, and to all that are afar off, even as many as the Lord our God shall call."

So, if one must believe anything about the post-conversion, post-water baptism, Holy Ghost baptism, the evidence points clearly in the direction that it is both relevant and universal. There is absolutely no scriptural basis to limit the experience to any particular age or generation.

SPEAKING IN TONGUES

But then, what about speaking in tongues? Some would agree up to this point concerning the Holy Ghost baptism but will refuse the accompanying evidence of speaking in tongues and prophecy. Some argue that tongues did not always accompany the Holy Ghost baptism in the Book of Acts in the Bible. Some also say that speaking in tongues is only one of the Holy Spirit's many gifts, and so should not be given undue prominence in the Church's experience and practice.

I did hold all these views in the past. But when I examined the weight of the evidence in Scripture, I changed my position on the matter.

There are six recorded reports of the experience of the baptism of the Holy Ghost in the Book of Acts. We find these in:

1. Acts 2:1– 4

2. Acts 4:31

3. Acts 8:14– 19

4. Acts 9: 17– 18

5. Acts 10:44– 48

6. Acts 19:1– 7

Let us look at these accounts very briefly:

ACTS 2:1–4

This passage was the first experience of the baptism of the Holy Ghost on the day of Pentecost. The account stated that both the apostles and the disciples who were present did speak in other tongues.

ACTS 4:31

This passage details the second experience of the baptism of the Holy Ghost among the early disciples. These people received the baptism earlier on the day of Pentecost, and they spoke in tongues. We can confidently say that this experience followed the persecution arising from the healing of the disabled person at the temple gate called beautiful. It was an answer to the threat they were facing. A new wave of Holy Ghost infilling was reassurance from heaven for the men and women under pressure (Luke 11:9-13).

ACTS 8:14– 19

This passage is the account of the experience of the Samaritan converts noted earlier. Some people argue that we are not told here expressly that there was an unusual manifestation. We are not told either that there was no manifestation of tongues and prophecy.

But suppose we study that passage very closely: We can infer that there must have been manifestations. Otherwise, Simon, the sorcerer, would not have been persuaded to offer money to acquire the power to bestow the gift. Although we cannot state that there were manifestations of tongues and prophecy in this experience in Samaria, we can conclude within reasonable doubts that there must have been manifestations.

ACTS 9: 17-18

The conversion of the Apostle Paul and how he received the Holy Ghost is detailed for us in this passage. Although the evidence of tongues and prophecy was not mentioned here, we have it on record from the apostle himself that he did speak in tongues extensively.

"I thank my God, I speak with tongues more than ye all."

—1 Corinthians 14:18.

Although the passage did not state that Paul did speak with tongues after Ananias laid hands on him in Acts 9, we are careful to note that tongues and prophecy accompanied his ministration of the same experience to the Ephesians in Acts 19 as manifestations. No wonder he said in 1 Corinthians 14:5: "I would *prefer* that ye all spake with tongues--"

ACTS 10:44-48

This passage is the experience in the house of the gentile convert Cornelius the centurion, a Roman military officer. It was here that speaking in tongues was used as a validation test, as we read in the following verses:

"While Peter yet spake these words, the Holy Ghost fell on all them which heard the word.

And they of the circumcision which believed were astonished as many as came with Peter because that on the Gentiles also was poured out the gift of the Holy Ghost."

How did they know that the Gentiles, too, had received the same gift?

"For they heard them speak with tongues, and magnify God" (Acts 10:46.)

These tongues and prophecy were the validation test for these Jewish converts as we hear Peter recount the experience in his report to the elders at Jerusalem in Acts 11:5, which says, "As I began to speak, the Holy Ghost fell on them as on us at the beginning."

ACTS 19:1-7

We have already referred to this passage earlier. The manifestations of tongues and prophecy accompanied the baptism of the Holy Ghost among these supposed disciples at Ephesus.

Out of six reports in the book of Acts, three clearly stated that the manifestation of speaking in other tongues accompanied the experience of Holy Ghost baptism. We find this in the accounts in Acts 2, 10, and 19.

In Acts 9, the Apostle Paul was the only one involved, and he, too, spoke in tongues extensively.

In Acts 4:31, the documented refilling experience was among those who had earlier received the Holy Ghost and had spoken in tongues in Acts 2.

So that makes five out of six reports.

The last one is the reported account in Samaria, Acts 8. As pointed out earlier, we can conclusively say that there were manifestations unusual enough to have persuaded Simon, the sorcerer, that it was worth paying to acquire the power to bestow the gift.

We may not argue with intense fervour that the Samaritans did speak with tongues. But we may argue with justification that since the usual manifestation of the receiving of the Holy Ghost was tongues and prophecy, the arguable but acceptable manifestation(s) of Acts 8 could not be expected to differ in content.

Be that as it may, we may conclude, again with reasonable justification, that manifestations did accompany the baptism of the Holy Ghost in all cases. This manifestation involved tongues in most of the cases reported in Scripture.

THE USE OF TONGUES

Having gone to this length to establish the case for the Holy Ghost's baptism for believers today with accompanying tongues and prophecy, the question then is: of what use is this tongue after all?

I believe that speaking in tongues in prayer does sharpen our spiritual sensibility. The Apostle Paul wrote in 1 Corinthians. 14:4 that, "He that speaketh in an unknown tongue edifieth himself... But he that prophesieth edifieth the Church."

In other words, tongues do for the individual, what prophecy does for the Church as a body.

When the Church is edified, it is built up in the inner man to walk in the Spirit (Galatians 5:25, Ephesians3:16).

The experience of those who pray in tongues regularly is the same. This benefit is also stated in the general epistle of Jude in verse 20, which says: "But ye beloved, building up yourselves on your most holy faith, praying in the Holy Ghost."

Praying in the Holy Ghost is one way we can build up ourselves in our most holy faith. And as we can readily see, praying in the Holy Ghost is, in fact, synonymous with praying in tongues: "For he that speaketh in an unknown tongue speaketh not unto men, but unto God; for no man understandeth him, howbeit in the spirit he speaketh mysteries" (1 Corinthians 14:2).

Again we read: "For if I pray in an unknown tongue, my spirit prayeth, but my understanding is unfruitful" (1 Corinthians. 14:2).

In Acts 2, we may note that the apostles spoke with other tongues on the day of Pentecost, but it was the Holy Spirit who gave them the utterance. "And they were all filled with the Holy Ghost, and spake with tongues, as the Spirit gave them utterance" (Acts 2:4).

As a result of all these, I concluded years ago that speaking in tongues regularly does sharpen our spiritual sensibilities for effective communion with God. While we are actively speaking in tongues, the Holy Spirit of God is continuously interacting with our spirit, sharpening our ability to sense Him at all times.

Again, since it is the Holy Spirit that gives the utterance when one is praying in tongues, there is a strong Scriptural basis to believe that praying in tongues is one sure way to pray in the will of God with or without our being aware of it.

"Likewise, the Spirit also helpeth our infirmities; for we know not what we should pray for as we ought; but the Spirit itself maketh intercession for us with groanings which cannot be uttered.

And he that searcheth the hearts knoweth what is the mind of the Spirit, because he maketh intercession for the saints ACCORDING TO the will of God.

—Romans 8:26-27

Finally, it may be necessary to encourage those who may be afraid that they may receive tongues from the devil if they desire the Holy Ghost's baptism with the manifestations of tongues and prophecy. One way to look at such a possibility, if indeed it is a possibility, is to put oneself in God's position as we consider this passage:

"If ye then being evil, know how to give good gifts unto your children: how much more shall your heavenly Father give the Holy Spirit to them that ask him.

—Luke 11:13

The truth is that the Almighty God is far better than us in giving good gifts to those who ask Him.

Ye are of God, little children, and have overcome them; because greater is he that is in you, than he that is in the world.

—1 John 4:4

The giver of the Holy Spirit is our Father in heaven, and He is the creator of all heaven and earth. The devil is one of His creatures, albeit a disobedient one. There can never be a comparison between the creator and His creature, never.

Therefore, I would like to believe that whenever I ask the Lord in my prayers to fill or refill me with the Holy Ghost, I will receive none other than the one and only Spirit of the Living God. The Holy Spirit will give my human spirit utterance to cause me to speak in tongues that I have never learned and to prophesy. As I do this daily, my spiritual sensibility sharpens for a more effective communion with the Spirit of God.

CHAPTER THREE

PRAYER

PREAMBLE

I f you picked up this book with a desire to learn how to pray, you may have by now been wondering when we would get to the subject.

The subject of prayer has a great deal to do with the new birth and developing our relationship with God. In Matthew 6:9-13 we read these words:

> After this manner therefore pray ye: Our father which art in heaven. Hallowed be thy name.
>
> Thy kingdom come. Thy will be done in earth, as it is in heaven.
>
> Give us this day our daily bread.
>
> And forgive us our debts, as we forgive our debtors.
>
> And lead us not into temptation, but deliver us from evil: For thine is the kingdom, and the power, and the glory forever. Amen.

OUR FATHER

The fact that Jesus started His teaching on prayer with these words: "Our Farther," underscores the great importance He attached to the relationship. It means that when a person is praying, he should speak as a child to his father. If a family has a good, warm, and intimate relationship, no child in such a circumstance would be a stranger to his father. There are a good number of people who remember their childhood with nostalgia. They recall the warm and intimate relationship that existed between them and their fathers.

As a physician I was privileged to watch such a relationship at very close quarters. Not too long ago I admitted an eighty-three-year old man with a failing kidney, into the hospital. I was later to learn that at the old man's eighty-third birthday celebration a few days earlier, he had warned his son that there would be no eighty-fourth. But his son would not hear of it. We did everything we possibly could to control the ailing kidney, but it would appear the old man was determined to go. But I was impressed by his son.

He and his wife kept vigil by this old man's bedside for seventy-two hours, night and day. He told me he wanted his father to be at least ninety. He said to me: "My father was my righthand man in everything I did." What a wonderful relationship.

Our Lord and Saviour Jesus Christ taught us to call God our Father. But there are people who have fathers with whom they were or are not really close or intimate. In such a situation, the word father only represents a biological relationship. There is no intimacy, no closeness.

In the same way, a person may kneel in prayer and call God Father, but may be fully aware that there is actually no intimacy, no relationship at all. As he says his prayers, he feels a dryness as he fishes for words, that is, what is usually referred to as appropriate words.

Some people don't even attempt to say any words of their own. They repeat words that have been written down by someone else that they consider appropriate. Sometimes they repeat the words each day as a daily prayer.

When we bring that sort of prayer life to the level of a human relationship, we see immediately how ridiculous it really is. Nobody can imagine a father-son relationship where the son comes to his father everyday and repeats the same words.

It is obvious that in circumstances like that, the son may repeat the words, but with his thoughts afar off on other things. The father will notice the lack of attention, which is the hallmark of the lack of depth of the relationship. Sometimes the relationship is actually nonexistent. What is there is a religious ritual. The individual does not really know God. He has been taught to say those words and he just keeps repeating them, without any feeling, hoping that wherever God is. He is supposed to be hearing them.

I once heard the story of a man who always kissed his wife before leaving home for work each morning. His wife always waited at the breakfast table in her place. The routine was regular. He woke up every morning and did his morning rituals, then settled down to his breakfast. After breakfast he would go back to his room, brush his teeth, pick up his briefcase, walk back to the dining room, bend over and kiss his wife, and then move to his car.

At one stage his wife felt that the whole exercise had become routine and dead. She decided to try it out. One day she asked her domestic help to sit at her usual seat. As sure as anything, her husband came out, bent over, kissed the domestic help, and was moving to the exit. It proved the fact that what he was doing was simply a routine. There was no life in it.

To many people prayer is like that. It is all routine. There is no relationship. Although they will readily agree that God is their Father in heaven, they do not really know Him. He is still an abstract: Something or someone out there in the void.

As we discussed in the earlier two chapters, it is only the new birth experience that can make the fatherhood of God a reality. God is a Spirit (John 4:24). We can only sense God with our human spirit, and until we are born again this human spirit is dead.

> But as many as received Him, to them gave He power [the authority] to become [call themselves, feel like] the sons of God, even to them that believe on His name:
> Which were born, not of blood, nor of the will of the flesh nor of the will of man [biological birth], but of God [spiritual birth].
> —John 1:12-13.

THY KINGDOM COME

It is not surprising that after our Lord Jesus had taught us the nature of the relationship we ought to have with Almighty God, He moved on to speak about the kingdom of God. "Thy kingdom come!"

The concept of the reality of the kingdom of God was greatly misunderstood by the Jews, including the disciples. All of them without exception had imagined that the kingdom of God was a physical kingdom, where men hold positions of responsibility and authority. But our Lord Jesus emphasized this in John 18:36 in His response to Pilate when He said, "My kingdom is not of this world: If My kingdom were of this world, then would My servants fight, that I should not be delivered to the Jews: but now is My kingdom not from hence."

Again, in His discussions on the parable of the sower our Lord Jesus also said in Mark 4:11, "Unto you it is given to know the mystery of the kingdom of God."

There are many people who say the Lord's prayer everyday without knowing the mystery of this kingdom they are praying to come. Our

Lord said to the Jews in Matthew 12:28, "But if I cast out devils by the Spirit of God, then the kingdom of God is come unto you."

Again He said in Luke 17:20-21 as follows:

And when He was demanded of the Pharisees, when the kingdom of God should come. He answered them and said, The kingdom of God cometh not with observation:
Neither shall they say, Lo here! or Lo there! for, behold, the kingdom of God is within you.

When, therefore, we kneel and pray, thy kingdom come, there are many who imagine a kingdom somewhere that should appear.

What our Lord Jesus was actually saying is that we should pray that men and women should begin to enter into the kingdom of God as the kingdom of God is established within them.

Thy kingdom come is therefore synonymous with the new birth experience. When a person is born again, the kingdom of God moves into his heart. His human spirit is awakened and so he begins to communicate with the Spirit of God. The kingdom of God moves within him and he begins to live as a child of the kingdom with kingdom rules and regulations.

This is why in Matthew 11:12 Jesus said, "And from the days of John the Baptist until now the kingdom of heaven suffereth violence, and the violent take it by force."

In other words, those who recognize the kingdom for what it is really worth, go all out to grab it, daring all obstacles of pride, fame, wealth, immorality, anger, hatred, education, et cetera.

We might therefore conclude by saying that for a person to truly pray to his Father in heaven, then he himself must belong to the kingdom of heaven. The kingdom must come within him. Otherwise he has no right whatsoever to pray to a Father in heaven.

THY WILL BE DONE

As part of our preamble to the discussion on prayer one of the aspects of the Lord's prayer that is pertinent is this one that says thy will be done on earth, as thy will is always done in heaven.

Again, when we say this prayer some of us imagine that our Lord Jesus was speaking of some organised society where the law is patterned according to the will of God.

It is obvious that this is not literally possible, as the will of God as revealed in His word often only provides the guiding principles for man and does not cover every single aspect of human conduct in an organised society.

But the will of God can be done as a matter of routine in the life of an individual.

When a person enters the kingdom of God by being born again, the next thing that should be done is the rigorous and relentless pursuit of the will of God in his or her life.

This is the singular most important reason why many peoples' experiences of the new birth remain stunted, without any growth. It is because they did not rigorously and tenaciously pursue and grab the will of God in their lives.

But our Lord Jesus put it in perspective. He said that after the kingdom must of necessity follow the will of God. To claim to have entered the kingdom without the conscious pursuit of the will of God is a contradiction.

"Thy kingdom come! Thy will be done." It is the active pursuit of the will of God that distinguishes the Christian faith from mere religion. The will of God as taught in the Bible is not a passive inadvertence. In other words, it is not just something that we fall back on each time we have no explanation. Some people will attribute every and any experience of theirs as the will of God. It will mean that our lives are preprogrammed and that there is nothing we can do actively or passively to alter the programme.

If that were to be the case, then our Lord Jesus would not have taught us to pray: Thy will be done on earth, as it is always done in heaven.

In fact, if we lived in heaven rather than on earth, we could justifiably say that anything that happens to us is the will of God. But since we live on earth and not in heaven, then we must pray for the will of God to be done.

The fact that we were urged to pray by our Lord tells us immediately that there must be things that are happening that are not the will of God, which we ought to pray to change. Our prayers are supposed to harness the forces of God to effect the will of God in our lives and circumstances.

But it is possible to simply pray for the will of God to be done in every situation. That may be good enough for a person outside the kingdom who does not really have a relationship with the Father in heaven.

If we think of a normal family relationship here on earth, it would be expected that a child would first find out from his father what he actually wants and then go ahead to see to it that what his father wants is what is done.

By the same token, the LORD God Almighty would expect His child to actively seek His will, find out what it is, and go ahead to execute it.

So, when our Lord Jesus taught us to pray, "Thy will be done," He was not providing us with an explanation for our every experience: He was rather inviting us to an active collaboration with Almighty God to effect His will on earth. And that presupposes that we have the capacity to sense the mind of our God.

In Romans 12:2, the Apostle Paul wrote: "And be not conformed to this world: But be ye transformed by the renewing of your mind, that you may prove what is that good, and acceptable, and perfect, will of God."

The will of God is something to be proved. In fact the suggestion here is that we must be careful to ensure that what we have accepted as the will of God is the perfect one. The inference here is that you can be fooled into accepting a counterfeit or imperfect one.

In Matthew 12:50 our Lord Jesus said, "For whosoever shall do the will of my Father which is in heaven, the same is my brother, and sister, and mother."

This particular passage is interesting from the point of view of perspectives. It implies that the will of God should be actively pursued. "Whosoever shall do the will of my father..." In other words, they ought to find it out on a daily basis and then do it.

The Apostle James actually implied in his own writing that the will of God should be the determining factor in a person's conduct, when he said, "For that ye ought to say, if the Lord will, we shall live, and do this, or that" (James 5:15).

Someone might then say, "Oh, yes, I agree. That is why anytime something happens, I always say that that is the way the Lord wants it." But suppose it is not, and that in fact, why it happened was because you did not know what God really wanted and so could not actively work for it?

Again because you did not actively work for what God wanted, what happened then had to happen, not as the perfect will of God, but as the outcome of the lack of effective pursuit of God's will.

Someone may also argue that, that implies that God is incapable of carrying out His will independent of us. The answer to that is a modified yes. What is more appropriate is that God is sometimes unwilling to carry out His will independent of us particularly when that will concerns us. That is why our Lord Jesus taught us to pray, "Thy will be done on earth." The obvious implication of that prayer is that God's will is not always done on earth as it is always done in heaven.

If we look at the life of our Lord and Saviour Jesus Christ, we would immediately see that it was completely dominated by the active pursuit of the will of God: "I can of my own self do nothing: as I hear, I judge. And my judgement is just; because I seek not my own will, but the will of the Father which hath sent me (John 5:30)."

Here, our Lord tells us clearly that He actively seeks the will of God. "As I hear, I judge." This answers those who will insist that the will of God can only be known in retrospect, and that it is never prospective. But we can see clearly that the teaching of the Bible is to the contrary.

This is why in the earlier chapters of this book on the new birth, we dwelt extensively on sensing the Spirit of God and being able to commune with God or better still, dialogue with God, as is revealed here in the statement: "As I hear, I judge."

THE CONCEPT OF GOD'S WILL AND PRAYER

Someone may ask, "What does the will of God haveto do with prayer?" The Bible says:
And this is the confidence that we have in Him, that if we ask anything according to His will. He heareth us:
And if we know that He hear us, whatsoever we ask, we know that we have the petitions that we desired of Him
—1 John 5:14-15.

This is the one passage that places the will of God in its most appropriate perspective with respect to prayer. "If we ask anything that is according to His will. He will hear us."

Someone may easily say, "Oh I now see why my prayer was not answered. It probably was not in His will."

Oftentimes this is an excuse for unbelief. And the enemy of our souls, the devil, loves to push us into that kind of corner and leave us there quarrelling with our Father about His will.

A man may wonder whether his request is in the will of God or not. He can stay wondering endlessly forever and ever.

If we judge from our experience and that of others we would see that it is often prayers that are not answered that are said not to be in the will of God. The implication of this is that every prayer that is answered must be in the will of God.

But when we look into the Bible more closely we find that, that position may not be quite correct.

In Numbers 22, we are told about the prophet Balaam who persuaded God to tell him what he wanted to hear. The end result of that encounter showed that the answer he got eventually was not in the will of God.

If a man is capable of sensing the Spirit of God, who transmits the mind of God to our human spirit as recorded in (1 Corinthians.2:11-12), then he would be able to know whether his prayer request should be made at all. James 4:3 says: "Ye ask, and receive not, because ye ask amiss, that ye may consume it upon your lusts."

If God approves of a prayer request before it is made, then faith is heightened and expectation follows naturally.

It is important to state here that the will of God in many areas of life is already revealed in the word of God.

For example, a person may not bother to ask whether it is the will of God to heal the sick? The Bible has already said: "Beloved I wish above all things that thou mayest prosper and be in health, even as thy soul prospereth" (3 John 2).

The will of God to heal us or to keep us in health, and prosper us materially, is already revealed. The one reason why many do not receive these blessings is that they often ignore the principles related to each of them. God's blessings overtake those who follow His principles for each blessing.

We shall deal with this subsequently when we touch on very common prayer needs.

In summary, we may conclude that when our Lord and Saviour Jesus Christ taught us to pray, "Thy will be done," He was teaching us the active pursuit of the will of God in our individual lives. Our Lord was in fact stating that we should insist on the will of God in prayer.

This offers a powerful anchor for faith. A man following the principles of God's word as it relates to a particular blessing may insist in prayer that the will of God as revealed be diligently pursued and effected in his life. This is the bedrock of importunity in prayer. It is based on the will of God. A person can be zealous for God's will in his life and so have his needs met by the Lord.

LEAD US NOT INTO TEMPTATION–BUILDING INTIMACY WITH GOD

The last concept we are going to deal with from our Lord's prayer as a preamble to our study on prayer is embodied in this thought —and lead us not into temptation.

It is very important to examine the expression that our Lord Jesus used when He called His disciples. It says a great deal to us when we realize that everybody that our Lord called, He had this to say to them: "follow me."

We all are called to follow Him. Nobody is called to lead. It is only those who have learned to follow Him closely that He allows to lead for in leading they only show others how to follow Him. The call is to follow Christ and not to come to Him with our own agenda.

But for people to follow intelligently, they must be able to communicate distinctly with the leader.

When our Lord Jesus taught us to pray, "And lead us not into temptation," He was only restating the principle of followership. His prayer injunction implies that if we are able to follow, God Almighty by His Holy Spirit would lead us away from the temptation that will make us to fail, and from the evil snares that the devil has placed on our path.

This principle of following God is the one great factor that builds intimacy with God. A person who is following God daily in every area of his or her life must be quite close to Him. This closeness builds so much intimacy that God's "wink" or "nod" is sensed and obeyed.

As followership is pursued rigorously in obedience, so the degree of intimacy grows.

Intimacy is at the heart of effective intercession. In Genesis 18:17-19 we read:

And the Lord said. Shall I hide from Abraham that thing which I do; Seeing that Abraham shall surely become a great and mighty nation, and all the nations of the earth shall be blessed in him?

For I know him, that he will command his children and his household after him and they shall keep the way of the Lord, to do justice and judgement; that the Lord may bring upon Abraham that which He hath spoken of him.

Abraham was called the friend of God. They were close. In this passage the Lord gives us insight into the basis of their intimacy. God says of Abraham, "I know the man. He will not only follow me, but he will get his whole household to do the same." This is the basis of God's intimate relationship with Abraham.

When we turn to Abraham's intercession on behalf of Sodom and Gomorrah, we are made to come face to face with the effective power of intimacy in prayer.

Some of us would consider Abraham's language rude (Genesis.18:23-25):

And Abraham drew near, and said. Wilt thou also destroy the righteous with the wicked?

Peradventure there be fifty righteous within the city: wilt thou also destroy and not spare the place for the fifty righteous that are therein?

That be far from thee to do after this manner, to slay the righteous with the wicked: and that the righteous should be as the wicked, that be far from thee: Shall not the judge of all the earth do right?

This is the height of audacity. "Shall not the judge of all the earth do right?" You may wonder: Can a mortal talk to the Almighty God like that?

The answer is simple: They were close, very close: very intimate indeed. They understood each other perfect-ly. We can see that in the reply in verse 26: "And the Lord said, if I find in Sodom fifty righteous within the city, then I will spare all the place for their sakes."

When we look at the next verse, we can sense that Abraham was conscious of not going too far. He knew they were close, yet he knew he still had to be careful. Verse 27 of the same chapter says: "And

Abraham answered and said, Behold, now, I have taken upon me to speak unto the Lord, which I am but dust and ashes."

He was reminding himself to be careful and be respectful, and not to abuse the privilege of intimacy. But the force of his argument was not diminished at all in verse 28:

Peradventure there shall lack of five of the fifty righteous: Wilt thou destroy all the city for lack of five?
And He [the Lord] said, if I find forty and five, I will not destroy it.?

Abraham was challenging God in prayer with what he knew about His nature, i.e. God's nature. He said to God, "No, Lord, You can't do that. You are a righteous God. It is unfair to destroy the righteous with the wicked and have them suffer the same fate." Only those who are close, really close, can speak with the Lord like that without condemnation in their spirit. Even in ordinary inter-human relationships people don't talk like that to their peers except when they are close. Even when they are close to those higher than they are in life, they would have to be really close, to talk like that as we shall see:

And he spake unto Him yet again, and said, perad-venture there shall be forty found there. And He [the Lord] said, I will not do it for forty's sake.
And he said unto Him, Oh let not the Lord be angry, and I will speak: peradventure there shall thirty be found there. And He said, I will not do it. If I find thirty there.
And he said, Behold, now, I have taken upon me to speak unto the Lord: Peradventure there shall be twenty found there. And He [the Lord] said, I will not destroy it for twenty's sake.

And he said. Oh let not the Lord be angry, and I will speak yet but this once: Peradventure ten shall be found there, and He said, I will not destroy it for ten's sake.

And the Lord went His way, as soon as He had left communing with Abraham: and Abraham returned unto his place.

—Genesis. 18:29–33

The interesting thing about this prayer of intercession is the way the deep relationship between Abraham and the Lord is revealed. As Abraham lowered the requisite number of righteous souls needed before the Lord could rescind His judgement, we see clearly that he was conscious of the fact that there was a limit.

When he moved from fifty to forty-five, he was quite bold about it. "Wilt thou destroy all the city for lack of five?"

When the Lord replied that five will not make a difference, Abraham realized that Sodom really had a problem. He decided to lower it by multiples of ten. "Lord, what about forty?" "Okay, I will spare it for forty's sake."

When Abraham was going to move from forty to thirty, he obviously realized that he was beginning to really tug on the strings of intimacy. That is why he paused to say: "Please excuse my liberty," in verse 30. "What about thirty?"

He moved cautiously from thirty to twenty. And when he realized twenty could still not be found, he told the Lord, "I will ask just this once only. What about ten?"

When the Lord said there are not up to ten righteous souls there, Abraham concluded that the case of Sodom was a very hopeless one. There was no need to go any further.

In fact, there were only four souls in Sodom: Lot, his wife, and his two daughters, just four. So that even if Abraham had gone down to five, Sodom would still have been destroyed. It is consistent with the nature of God that the four righteous souls were first rescued before the city was destroyed.

In conclusion, it is important to note that developing an intimate relationship with the Lord is the bedrock of effective prayer. As we shall see later, prayer becomes natural and conversational: No special words, no special phrases: Just plain simple and natural conversation.

Our Lord Jesus taught us to pray: "And lead us not into temptation."

In Romans 8:14 we read: "For as many as are led by the Spirit of God, they are the sons of God."

We can see immediately why we stated unequivocally earlier that sensing the Spirit of God is the next most important thing to the new birth. It is by listening and obeying the Lord that we develop a very intimate relationship with Him, which will make praying very effective. Besides, the assurance derived there from becomes an added booster to our faith as we journey through life.

CHAPTER FOUR

ESSENTIAL PRINCIPLES

*A*nd it came to pass, that, as He was praying in a certain place, *when He ceased, one of His disciples said unto Him, Lord teach us to pray, as John taught his disciples. — Luke 11:1*

The question about prayer has very little to do with forms and manners, but it has a great deal to do with principles.

When someone says, "I do not know how to pray," he or she may be referring to forms and patterns. They may have heard some particular words used by others. For some, it may be inflections of voice and cadence. Others may be worried about saying the wrong thing theologically.

Often, when some people pray in public, they exhibit their knowledge of the Bible deliberately and intimidate those who are not so versed in the Bible and who, as a result, refuse to pray publicly. Sometimes, such use of the Bible is a genuine effort by the person praying to lift his faith and others' faith to unite their hearts together in their intercession. But the person who says he does not know how to pray is nonetheless intimidated. They have come to associate effective prayer with the ability to use Bible references.

The use of Bible references to build up faith in prayer is something to be encouraged. The reason is that the Lord answers prayers according to His exceeding good and precious promises, by which we are made partakers of the divine nature, according to 2 Peter 1:4. But that is not to say that those who have not learned a good deal of these Bible verses cannot pray effectively.

When our Lord Jesus taught us to pray to our Father in heaven, He expected us to talk, honestly and naturally. He expected us to come to God as a child comes to his father, trusting that He would accept us through His Son, our savior.

COMING BEFORE GOD

There are some useful principles to deal with when a person comes to God in prayer.

FEELING OF UNWORTHINESS

Some people say: "God can't hear a person like me. Hey, I know who I am. I know I am rotten through and through, and there is just no way a Holy God can stop to listen to a person like me."

This attitude is often a very natural feeling that sometimes reflects the real depth of sin in which the person is living. To avoid being hypocritical, he turns his back on God and prefers not to pray at all.

It is not only people who have not experienced the new birth that have this feeling. Sometimes even people who have experienced the new birth are turned off praying because of one sin or the other in their lives or something they are doing or have done wrong.

This question is a sore point with agnostics and atheists. Some believe that this is the greatest undoing of society, the fact that a person can believe in the forgiveness of sins. "Because they believe they can be forgiven, that is why they make no genuine effort to change their ways," they contend.

The feeling of unworthiness can be erased in us by a deep appreciation of God's love in Christ Jesus for the sinner. This love sent our Lord Jesus to the Cross of Calvary to die for the sins of all humanity. But what many have failed to appreciate is that cleansing from sin through the Blood of Jesus is conditional: "But if we walk in the light, as He is in the light, we have fellowship one with another, and the blood of Jesus Christ His Son cleanses us from all sin." (1 John 1:7).

To walk in the light of God's word is a preserve, if not privilege of those who have come to God through Christ. These are those individuals who are born again. It is only in the process of being born again that the blood of Jesus can cleanse us from all sins. God provides cleansing for sin through the blood of Jesus: "In whom [Jesus] we have redemption through His blood, the forgiveness of sins according to the riches of His grace." (Ephesians 1:7).

Many have wondered why anybody's sin should be forgiven at all. Some have argued that the concept of forgiveness through grace is untenable. A man should be made accountable for his sins, not forgiven. They may not know that forgiveness is offered to humanity in Christ through judicial pardon to raise a group of believers that work righteousness out of gratitude and love. 2 Corinthians 5:14-15 (NLT2)

"Either way, Christ's love controls us. Since we believe that Christ died for all, we also believe that we have all died to our old life.

"He died for everyone so that those who receive his new life will no longer live for themselves. Instead, they will live for Christ, who died and was raised for them.

It was to answer the logic of this thinking that the Apostle Paul wrote: "For the Jews require a sign, [i.e., that there is redemption and forgiveness in Christ] and the Greeks [i.e., Gentile philosophers and thinkers] seek after wisdom" (i.e., the logic of the whole point).

"But we preach Christ crucified, (i.e., the shed blood on the cross of Calvary) unto the Jews a stumbling block, and unto the Greeks foolishness" (1Corinthians 1:22–23).

But to answer the question of the blood and the feeling of unworthiness before the Lord, we must think in terms of God's eternal laws. We find this in the Book of Leviticus stated in absolute terms: "For the life of the flesh is in the blood: and I have given it to you upon the altar to make an atonement for your souls: For it is the blood that maketh atonement for the soul" (Leviticus 17:11).

Again, in Hebrews 9:22, the Bible restates this point: "And almost all things are by the law purged with blood, and without shedding of blood is no remission."

To appreciate this fully, one needs to see the whole scenario from God's perspective.

God is Holy (1 Peter 1:15). The holiness of God is absolute. God, by nature, cannot tolerate sin. But God must of necessity relate with the man whom He has created in His image.

To God, sin is really like treason. And anyone who sins deserves to die. That is why in Romans 6:23, the Bible states: "For the wages of sin is death: but the gift of God is eternal life through Jesus Christ our Lord."

For a person who has sinned to continue to have fellowship with a holy God, he must find a substitute to die in his place each time he sins.

In the Old Testament, God allowed the people to use a lamb without blemish as their substitute.

But the practice degenerated into a ritual. The ritual overshadowed the spiritual significance of reconciliation with God. So people then felt that so long as they performed the ritual, God should be satisfied. He should not be bothered about the wrong things they were doing so long as they performed the ceremony.

It is as a result of this kind of degenerate thinking that we find God speaking to the people through the prophets in this vein:

"To what purpose *is* the multitude of your sacrifices to Me?" Says the LORD."I have had enough of burnt offerings of rams And the fat of fed cattle. I do not delight in the blood of bulls, Or of lambs or goats.

"When you come to appear before Me, Who has required this from your hand, To trample My courts?

"Bring no more futile sacrifices; Incense is an abomination to Me. The New Moons, the Sabbaths, and the calling of assemblies-- I cannot endure iniquity and the sacred meeting.

"Your New Moons and your appointed feasts My soul hates; They are a trouble to Me, I am weary of bearing *them.*"

—Isaiah 1:11-14 (NKJV)

It is most unfortunate that many of us do not appreciate how much God hates religion. By religion, I mean the rituals. God thoroughly hates religious practices that are devoid of any spiritual relationship. "And when ye spread forth your hands, I will hide mine eyes from you: yea, when ye make many prayers, I will not hear: your hands are full of blood." (Isaiah 1:15).

The concept of religion as an end in itself has always been man's idea. It is corruption, the exploitation that is often for selfish purposes. The Prophet continues:

"Wash you; make you clean; put away the evil of your doings from before mine eyes, cease to do evil;

"Learn to do well; seek judgment, relieve the oppressed, judge the fatherless, plead for the widow."

—Isaiah 1:16-17

When religion is an instrument for a spiritual awakening, then the Almighty God is interested. If religion is an instrument to a God-fearing life, then He will send His quickening grace. But where religious practices are the end in themselves or seen as a gift to appease God, the Bible states that the ritual would be abhorrent before Him.

But contrary to those who say that God must mete out punishment according to the law of retributive justice, the Prophet contends that where there is a genuine spiritual awakening towards a God-fearing and God-centered life, God is quite willing to forgive the past.

"Come now, and let us reason together, saith the Lord: though your sins be as scarlet, they shall be as white as snow, though they be red like crimson, they shall be as wool.

"If ye be willing and obedient, ye shall eat the good of the land."

—Isaiah 1:18-19

HOW MANY TIMES SHOULD ONE REPENT?

This question is a very sore point with many people. On the one hand, some moralists and humanists believe that the concept of repetitive repentance makes a farce of religion.

But we see in the Bible the great love of God in accepting His creation's imperfections and weaknesses. He is careful not to provide an excuse for sin for those who have experienced a genuine spiritual awakening in Christ, which we call the new birth.

"What shall we say then? Shall we continue in sin, that grace may abound?

God forbid! How shall we, that are dead to sin [i.e., insensitive to the attractions of sinful lusts] live any longer therein?

—Romans 6:1-2

"Likewise reckon ye also yourselves to be dead indeed unto sin, [i.e., regard yourselves as people who are dead or insensitive to the attractions of sin] but alive unto God through Jesus Christ our Lord [i.e., sensitive only to the Spirit of God through Christ]. For he that is dead is freed from sin.

—Romans 6:7,11

The way the Bible puts it is that when a man has experienced a genuine spiritual awakening through Christ Jesus, which we call the new birth, he might still be struggling initially with a lot of his misdeeds.

But as he studies the word of God, the Spirit of God uses the word of God to re-establish the authority of his human spirit over his flesh (i.e. soul, and body). The attractions of the spirit life or God's life will take progressive precedence over the soul and body (Hebrews 4:12). The Apostle Peter made this point to young Christians when he wrote in 1 Peter 2:2: "As newborn babes, desire the sincere milk of the word, that you may grow thereby."

The Apostle Paul in his letter to the Hebrews, chapter 5, verse 12 lamented the lack of progress in the spiritual development of some of the converts: "For when for the time ye ought to be teachers, ye have need that one teach you again which be the first principles of the oracles of God; and are become such as have need of milk, and not of strong meat."

Maturity is distinct from perfection because nobody ever arrives at the state where he does not do anything wrong at all? Being born again is not being perfect. We all who have come to Christ are on a daily march to perfection. We never arrive until we see Him face to face at His appearing. The Bible states this clearly in 1 John 3:1-3:

[1] Behold what manner of love the Father has bestowed on us, that we should be called children of God! Therefore, the world does not know us, because it did not know Him.

[2] Beloved, now we are children of God; and it has not yet been revealed what we shall be, but we know that when He is revealed, we shall be like Him, for we shall see Him as He is.
[3] And everyone who has this hope in Him purifies himself, just as He is pure.
[4] Whoever commits sin also commits lawlessness, and sin is lawlessness.
[5] And you know that He was manifested to take away our sins, and in Him there is no sin.
[6] Whoever abides in Him does not sin. Whoever sins has neither seen Him nor known Him.
[7] Little children, let no one deceive you. He who practices righteousness is righteous, just as He is righteous.
[8] He who sins is of the devil, for the devil has sinned from the beginning. For this purpose the Son of God was manifested, that He might destroy the works of the devil.
[9] Whoever has been born of God does not sin, for His seed remains in him; and he cannot sin, because he has been born of God.
[10] In this the children of God and the children of the devil are manifest: Whoever does not practice righteousness is not of God, nor *is* he who does not love his brother.

—1 John 3:1-10 (NKJV)

The Apostle John is saying, in other words, that when a man is born again through faith in Jesus Christ, he becomes a child of God. He must subsequently commence a continuous purging exercise to get rid of sins in his life. This purging is the exercise that is completed in each one of us at the appearing of Christ at His second coming. As a child of God with the seed of God or the life of God in him, he will no longer sin wilfully or with premeditation. If a person is purportedly born again and continues to sin willfully, then he is not controlled by the Spirit of God but rather by the devil.

But many may wonder how possible it is to maintain absolute consistency and always have behaviour that tends to good and righteousness rather than evil. The Holy Spirit is both the answer and the solution to this struggle. The truth of the matter is that we never set out to be perfect. We set out to follow and obey the Holy Spirit in our lives. Whatever good revealed in our character is a fruit of that obedience. However, we are likely to miss the mark here and there now and again. But as increasing grace perfects our compliance, so does our errors diminish. Admittedly, no one can ever be error-free in this world.

What is essential to know is that when we miss the mark, we must go back and get cleansed again in the blood of Jesus. We attain to being blameless, which is the very best on this side of eternity, through periodic cleansing in the blood of Jesus.

A person that is born again is given a covering called the garment of righteousness. This garment is the righteousness of Christ that imputes perfection to imperfect people like you and me. Covered with this garment of righteousness, we can appear before God in heaven entirely blameless and unblameable. Colossians 1:21-22 (NKJV)

"And you, who once were alienated and enemies in your mind by wicked works, yet now He has reconciled "in the body of His flesh through death, to present you holy, and blameless, and above reproach in His sight--"

When a believer engages in spiritual warfare, this garment of righteousness becomes the breastplate of righteousness to constitute the final wall of defense in the Christian's armor. Sin unconfessed and uncleansed becomes a weak spot in this breastplate of righteousness. It also forms a zone of vulnerability. We learn to repent and cleanse ourselves in the blood of Jesus to renew the integrity of our breastplate of righteousness. 1 John 1:9 (NKJV)

"If we confess our sins, He is faithful and just to forgive us *our* sins and to cleanse us from all unrighteousness."

When we have the right attitude to godliness as Christians, we live daily, determined to stay away from all unrighteousness. The Apostle John addressed the question of slip-ups in life in his letter:

"My little children, these things write I unto you that you sin not. And if any man sin, we have an advocate with the Father, Jesus Christ the righteous:

"And He is the propitiation for our sins: and not for ours only, but also for the sins of the whole world.

—1 John 2:1-2

"In summary, the feeling of unworthiness leads to tremendous ineffectiveness in prayer. The approach is beggarly. Faith cannot operate because there is a deep sense of guilt and inadequacy.

It is to eliminate this feeling of unworthiness in prayer that the Apostle John wrote, "If we confess our sins, He is faithful and just to forgive us our sins, and to cleanse us from all unrighteousness" (1 John 1:9).

The implication is that when we genuinely repent of our sins, the blood of Jesus as our substitute will cleanse us from every sin. In other words, the blood of Jesus is the "detergent" with which to wipe away the spots of sin on our garment of righteousness so that it will become spotlessly clean again.

It is important to note that the Bible's position is that the blood cleanses us from all sin.

Some feel that their sin is such that nothing can wipe it away. But you had better believe it as you read this. God has said that the blood of Jesus will wipe any and every sin. This assurance is what confers boldness as we approach God in prayer.

A man that is thoroughly cleansed by the blood is wholly clean and can appear before his God very confidently, knowing that the God of heaven and earth will accept him.

The Bible describes this as the riches of His grace (unmerited favor) in Ephesians 1:7.

It is a pity of religion and religious practices that this constant cleansing, a sensitivity to the Spirit of God, and His condemnation of sin (something often referred to as the pricking of the conscience) is done on particular days and particular occasions.

If a man, for instance, tells a lie in the course of his interaction with his fellow man, he should immediately reach out to the Lord for forgiveness and, where necessary, make restitution. He does not have to wait until he arrives at a confessional service on a Thursday or church on a Sunday to get right with the Lord. It is freedom or liberty to know that we can repent and be released from our sins anywhere and anytime.

GENUINE REPENTANCE

It may be inappropriate to conclude this question of the feeling of unworthiness during prayer without dealing with the question of what constitutes genuine repentance.

From the Bible position, wherever and whenever there is genuine repentance, God will always forgive sin (1 John 1:9).

What then constitutes genuine repentance? Some would say that sincere repentance is to be genuinely sorry for what one has done wrong.

But one can be genuinely sorry one hundred times a day, and there will be no question about the genuineness of the remorse. What may be recognizable is total incapacitation. It could also be outright possession that requires the ministration of deliverance from the enslaving power.

The Apostle Paul had to deal with the problem of incest in the Corinthian Church. In his first letter to them, as recorded in 1 Corinthians 5, he was unequivocal about his condemnation of the act. In his second letter to them, as recorded in 2 Corinthians 7, he took the opportunity to expound on the concept of genuine repentance.

"I am no longer sorry that I sent that letter to you, though I was very sorry for a time, realizing how painful it would be to you. But it hurt you only for a little while.

"Now I am glad I sent it, not because it hurt you, but because the pain turned you to God. It was a good kind of sorrow you felt, the kind of sorrow God wants His people to have so that I need not come to you with harshness.

"For God sometimes uses sorrow in our lives to help us turn away from sin and seek eternal life. We should never regret His sending it. But the sorrow of the man who is not a Christian is not the sorrow of true repentance and does not prevent eternal death.

"Just see how much good this grief from the Lord did for you! You no longer shrugged your shoulders but became earnest and sincere and very anxious to get rid of the sin about which I wrote to you. You became frightened about what had happened and longed for me to come and help. You went right to work on the problem and cleared it up (punishing the man who sinned). You have done everything you could to make it right."

—2 Corinthians. 7:8-11, (Living Bible)

The most significant and most crucial point about genuine repentance is not the sorrow but turning away from evil. The sadness is essential, but it is meaningless if it does not lead away from a life of sin.

One of the best examples of repentance in the Bible is the Ninevites' story detailing their corporate repentance, as recorded in the Bible Book of Jonah.

The Prophet Jonah arrived on their shores with a classical fire and brimstone judgemental sermon. He cried out in the market square, "Forty days only, and Nineveh will be destroyed." The result of that sermon was astounding:

"So the people of Nineveh believed God, proclaimed a fast and put on sackcloth, from the greatest of them even to the least of them.

"For word came unto the king of Nineveh, and he arose from his throne, and he laid aside his robe, and covered him with sackcloth, and sat in ashes.

"And he caused it to be proclaimed and published throughout Nineveh by the decree of the king and his nobles, saying, Let neither man nor beast, herd nor flock, taste anything: let them not feed, nor drink water.

"But let man and beast be covered with sackcloth, and cry mightily to God: yea, let them turn every one from his evil way, and from the violence that is in their hands."

—Jonah 3:5- 8

The vital thing about repentance is the turning away from evil, and where genuine sorrow for sin is followed by a turning away from the evil in question, God will always forgive.

The blood of Jesus sprinkled on our hearts will always make us bold to appear before His holy presence.

"Having, therefore, brethren, boldness to enter into the holiest by the blood of Jesus."

—Hebrews 10:19

"Let us draw near with a true heart in full assurance of faith, having our hearts sprinkled from an evil conscience, and our bodies washed with pure water."

—Hebrews 10:22

THANKSGIVING AND PRAISE

It is not uncommon for the pressures of need and time to rush us into God's presence with our requests. Often we are so overwhelmed by our burden that we approach the throne with bitterness and murmurings, complaining about our lot and the pressures we have to bear.

Some may even have approached the throne in open rebellion, blaming the Lord for the misfortunes or hurtful experiences that have overtaken them.

There is one good thought that always engenders praise as we approach the presence of God. I have always been encouraged to confront my seeming impossibilities with these beautiful words of Jesus:"... With men it is impossible, but not with God: for with God all things are possible."

When a person under severe pressure stops to meditate on the omnipotence of God to the degree that it permeates and dominates his waking thoughts, then he would be able to approach the throne of grace with thanksgiving and praise.

"Enter into His gate with thanksgiving, and into His courts with praise: be thankful unto Him and bless His name.

"For the Lord is good: His mercy is everlasting; and His truth endureth to all generations."

—Psalm 100:4-5

Most people would readily agree that we should enter God's presence with thanksgiving and praise, but they are often short of words. They fish for words to express their love for God and sometimes find that words are inadequate. This occasion is where being able to speak in tongues comes in very handy.

Some do not know what to say. These are the people who feel that there is a particular way to say it. But there is no specific way to say thank you when a relationship is intimate. The communication becomes informal but respectful.

THE PLACE OF SONGS

One way to enter His gates with thanksgiving and into His courts with praise is through songs, whether they be hymns or choruses.

Songs have a great place in corporate worship, where a good worship session lifts the soul in adoration of our God. It also has a great place in individual worship, especially where there is some quiet, and one can sing meditatively.

Besides using songs, an individual can enter God's presence with hearty greetings of thanksgiving and praise recounting with a deep sense of gratitude the things the Lord has done for him.

CHAPTER FIVE

THEY THAT WAIT UPON THE LORD

It is appropriate in this all-important chapter to examine the import of certain Scriptures and see whether we can glean the "art," if there is any such thing, of proper aggressive and meaningful praying.

Some years ago, I came across a rather interesting Christian poster. It showed a traffic sign that read, 'NO WAITING.' But they that wait upon the Lord shall renew their strength.

The person who inspired that poster probably must be well accustomed to the rush-rush lifestyle we live in today. Sometimes this is not of our own making. We are in a system that forbids us to slow down at all, even for one minute.

As a private medical practitioner living on my hospital premises and running a twenty-four-hour-a-day service, I got calls for emergencies, calls for non-emergencies, and sometimes for trivialities. It was difficult, if not impossible, to talk about an arranged day. Nothing was predictable. I could be called at 2 a.m., 4 a.m. 6 a.m., 10 a.m., 12 noon, 4 p.m., 6 p.m, 10 p.m. All round the clock. Some days to even eat was a great struggle.

My life, which hitherto had an organized routine of a one-hour prayer and meditation vigil between 5.am.and 6.a.m. was utterly disorganized. On top of that, I kept getting invitations to teach and preach, which the Lord would not allow me to turn down.

In the middle of all this confusion, the relevance of something I had learned years ago dawned on me. It is the place and beauty of conversational prayer. I recall arriving at a teaching Sunday meeting on the new anointing for college students, totally physically exhausted. I had driven the one hundred-odd kilometers to the school myself because my one driver was off on Sunday. He, too, was always exhausted.

All this happened in our practice's early days because we had no money to hire more staff.

As I arrived at the school premises, exhausted and without a sermon or sermon notes, I whispered up to the Lord and said: "Lord, You know what these students expect You to do for them. Please do it for us all. Don't count on me. Just help me to lean on Your precious Holy Ghost so You can feel my weight of dependence." I don't remember the exact words of that prayer, but it was words to that effect.

As I approached the auditorium where this meeting was going to hold, I met two students on their way to a confirmation service organized by their Church denomination.

I took the opportunity to tell them how my confirmation experience years ago meant nothing much to me afterward, save the privilege of now taking holy communion with older adults, including my parents. It was more of a religious obligation rather than a spiritual encounter. I looked forward to the Bishop laying his hands on me on that solemn occasion. I recall I left the service a sober person, rather than a changed person. My soberness did not last a long time before it was all eroded again by the pressures of life at school.

They agreed with me and decided they wanted a personal experience with Jesus. We prayed together, and I urged them to join the college Christian fellowship after their confirmation.

But the event of that day left me with an all-important experience of walking with God; It deposited vital nuggets, particularly in the area of depending on His Holy Spirit.

As the sermon progressed, I kept in touch with God through conversational prayer. He asked me to talk to the people about obstacles to a new anointing in their lives: envy and jealousy and the like, especially the need to be reconciled.

"If you have ought against anyone," I intoned, "you must make your peace now before we begin to pray for the new anointing." I called all of them out in front, and they came.

Then the Holy Spirit took over with conviction, and the people started to weep and moan and cry. It was a scene indeed as they made their peace with God and man. Then God told me that some people were holding out. As I told them, two more people joined them. Then God said there was still one more person, but I shouldn't wait for him. I asked the young man to be sure that he made his peace with God and man that day before the service ended.

When the weeping and the confessions were over, God said to me, "Son, it's time to pray for the new anointing."

We sang a song, and I began to pray for the people without touching anyone. I was praying out front there. Then the Holy Spirit took over the auditorium as the anointing of the Lord swept through the congregation.

I was amazed. More so because some people who fell under the anointing in some other meeting confided they thought the preacher pushed them down.

That complaint made me somewhat wary of using the "falling experience" as the only evidence of the Holy Ghost's movement. I decided not to lay hands on people often unless the Lord asks me to, and when I do lay hands, I make sure their heads are quite erect and their bodies quite straight so that if they buckled and fell, it wouldn't be because I caused it.

As a result of this, I only witnessed a few people falling in my meetings hitherto. I even recall a lady who loved the idea of falling during meetings as I perceived it in my spirit. Maybe she felt like doing me a favor as she noticed that people were not falling as I prayed for them. She rushed to me, and before I even got to pray, she was panting and slid to the floor prostrate. I was very suspicious. As I glanced at her a few minutes later, she was already back at her seat. She must have felt: "Poor preacher. I think someone needs to help him to look great and feel great."

That day was unique. The wave of anointing blew quite a few people over in the auditorium; young men and women. This move went on for a long time. We could not stop the meeting for hours.

I handed over the meeting to the fellowship leader, and they were still falling all over the hall. He tried to stop the service but also failed. The Lord was still dealing with the people.

As I reviewed the whole meeting, which admittedly was my greatest experience of the manifestation of the outpouring of the Spirit on the people till that date, I was amazed at the Lord and His ways.

Here was I exhausted, arriving for my meeting without a sermon, yet when I acknowledged my total unpreparedness, the Lord gave me precise instructions as to what to do.

As I went ahead and did them, the Holy Ghost moved upfront to bless the people. Waiting on the Lord must be understood by every believer who wants to function step by step with the Holy Ghost.

Some years ago, I had believed that waiting on the Lord implied that we must stop somewhere, often in fasting and praying to hear what the Lord had to say to us.

This narrow view of waiting on the Lord forced me to come to some meetings feeling that the Lord would not do much that day because I had not had enough time to wait on Him in fasting and praying with my sermon notes all worked out in detail.

As the Lord watched me struggle with this narrow view of waiting, He spoke to me one day, saying: "Son, I want you to preach without notes from now on until I say so."

I was worried about that initially. How can I preach without notes? Will I be able to organize my thoughts properly and make sense to the people? I had preached without notes occasionally before. But there was always an outline, some sketch of where I was going. But the Lord's instructions were that I had to trust Him for the passage and the message.

It proved a tremendous blessing and a good preparation for those intervening years in my life when I would have no time at all to write notes even if I wanted to.

I learned to listen and preach and trust the Lord for the outcome. I was amazed at how the Lord ministered to the people in many of these meetings. It was simply outstanding.

It was after these experiences that I started to learn how to wait on Him. He said that waiting involved total dependence. Sometimes you may have time to wait physically and meditate, and some other times, you have to wait on Him along the way, depending totally on Him every step of the way.

The only reason why some people may not be able to do this is if they are yet to develop the habit of conversational prayer. This form of prayer is the communion or dialogue that keeps us following our 'Guide' in realtime.

There are times we pray, and we tell God the way things are to unburden our hearts. But we should always remember the words of Scripture: "The Holy Spirit intercedes for the saints according to the will of God." (Romans 8:27)

Let us take a practical example of the temptation of lust. I believe the admonition of the Apostle Peter puts the temptation of lust in its most appropriate perspective: "Dearly Beloved, I beseech you as strangers and pilgrims, abstain from fleshly lusts which war against the soul"

—1 Peter 2:11

Here we find the precision in God's word revealed in great magnificence. Fleshly lusts have nothing to do with the spirit in man. They have a great deal to do with the soul.

As we said earlier, the soul has three parts: The will, the intellect, and the emotions.

Fleshly lusts naturally attack the emotions. The natural man will use his will to suppress the feelings and keep them in check. The lusts are still there, but because he is strong-willed at the time, he can resist the pressure.

But suppose for some reason, he is not so strong-willed, but rather he is tired and, in fact, exhausted physically? Suppose he is also highly vulnerable by being emotionally drained, then his strong will may sag. He may have taken some alcohol, too, and weakened his will and resolve.

His intellect can come to his rescue. He may tell himself that he is stupid to entertain such thoughts, knowing that he is now born-again. This struggle may go on for a while, and then occasionally, he finds that he cannot contain the torrent of emotions. The war in his soul practically drains him of spiritual energy that he is almost unable to approach God without a sense of guilt.

It is in this state that some fall into sin. When they do, the intellect may rationalize their predicament and urge them to repent, pleading the weakness of the flesh. If the will has recovered, they may pick up the struggle again, and the ding-dong affair goes on endlessly.

But this is not the way the Bible teaches us to fight sin. Let us continue with the problem of lust. The apostle Peter tells us it wars against the soul, not against the human spirit. The soul, therefore, is the battleground as we read in Galatians 5:16 & 17:

"This, I say then, walk in the spirit, and ye shall not fulfil the lust of the flesh. For the flesh lusteth [warreth] against the spirit, and the spirit against the flesh: and these are contrary the one to the other; so that ye cannot do the things that ye would."

The man who fights as outlined above with will power has not allowed the Holy Spirit to unleash His power against the war in his soul. He struggled to contain them through the exercise of self-will and his intellect.

Here is what the Scriptures say in Romans 8:12-14 (NRSV)

"So then, brothers and sisters, we are debtors, not to the flesh, to live according to the flesh—"for if you live according to the flesh, you will die; but if by the Spirit you put to death the deeds of the body, you will live.

"For all who are led by the Spirit of God are children of God.

In Galatians 5:18 we read: "But if ye be led of the spirit, ye are not under the law."

So, let us see how we can pray in a distressing situation like this. The crucial thing is that the Holy Spirit is at the centre of the solution to this challenge. The first thing is that the Holy Spirit is the one who can put these spiritually unhealthy passions to death. The second thing is that it is the same Holy Spirit that can lead us away from temptations that expose us to these pressures. So how do we achieve both objectives with conversational prayer?

There are specific goals we must note. To be free from the pressures of sin, a man must move from being dead in sin to being dead to sin. So, the first request in prayer is, "O LORD my God, I desire to be dead to sin. May Your Holy Spirit mortify my flesh that I may be free. I acknowledge the Scripture that says that he that is dead is free (Romans 6:7).

The second prayer is to acknowledge now and confess that you are dead to sin. We have this on the authority of Scripture too: Romans 6:11-13 (NRSV)

"So, you also must consider yourselves dead to sin and alive to God in Christ Jesus.

"Therefore, do not let sin exercise dominion in your mortal bodies to make you obey their passions.

"No longer present your members to sin as instruments of wickedness, but present yourselves to God as those who have been brought from death to life, and present your members to God as instruments of righteousness.

When I declare that I am dead to sin by choice, I invite the Holy Spirit to work that mystical death in me to kill the desire or the lust for sinful things. It is amazing how this happens. The controlling factor is sincerity. If the desire to be dead to sin is sincere, the Holy Spirit will trigger the mortification. And what happens is that we wake up to the realization one day that the power to attract us to sin is no longer there and that we are free. Besides, the struggle between the will and the passions does not exist within any longer.

Interestingly, the new task is to refocus my mind to redirect my body to function as a vessel or tool for righteousness as revealed in Romans 6:16-18 (NRSV)

16 Do you not know that if you present yourselves to anyone as obedient slaves, you are slaves of the one whom you obey, either of sin, which leads to death, or of obedience, which leads to righteousness?

17 But thanks be to God that you, having once been slaves of sin, have become obedient from the heart to the form of teaching to which you were entrusted,

18 and that you, having been set free from sin, have become slaves of righteousness.

There is no point in passing through the lust corridor repeatedly. We risk reigniting the passions that used to enslave us. And that is why we yield to the guidance of the Holy Spirit as revealed in Romans 8:14 (NRSV)

"For all who are led by the Spirit of God are children of God."

There is a part of the Lord's prayer that says: "And lead us not into temptation, but deliver us from evil." (Matthew 6:11) This prayer is crucial to staying away from sin. The Holy Spirit knows where snares are lurking. When we ask Him to guide and direct us in detail, we discover that we can avoid the devil's many pitfalls, traps, and tricks.

For those who are enjoying this mortification of the flesh by the Holy Spirit, the psalmist has five relevant prayers to share with you and me: Psalm 119:33-37 (NRSV)

33 Teach me, O LORD, the way of your statutes, and I will observe it to the end.

³⁴ Give me understanding that I may keep your law and observe it with my whole heart.

³⁵ Lead me in the path of your commandments, for I delight in it.

³⁶ Turn my heart to your decrees, and not to selfish gain.

³⁷ Turn my eyes from looking at vanities; give me life in your ways.

Such focused prayers serve to keep our thoughts and feelings away from sin and riveted on the ways of godliness and truth.

Nobody should fight sin with will power and intellect. They are not sufficiently equipped to achieve a permanent victory. Only the Holy Spirit knows the way to achieve a permanent victory through the mortification of the flesh. So the conversational prayer may begin somewhat like this:

Lord, I am sorry, I allowed these sinful thoughts to dwell too long in my heart (James 1:14-15).

That is where I made the first mistake. I shouldn't have watched that movie or read that book or flipped through that magazine.

I should have switched off when I saw it was not edifying to my soul. When we express these thoughts in prayer, identifying our previous errors, we confirm that we desire our flesh and its lustful passions to remain dead. The Holy Spirit will complete the task with such a sincere approach.

Sometimes, the full mortification of the flesh may take a while in coming. Under such circumstances, conversational prayer helps us keep away from temptations and situations that we cannot handle.

"O Lord, please help me to stay on the road that is straight and narrow today. Is there anything I am about to embark on that can trip me up? Please show me and strengthen me to stay focused and godly. This is how we can pray all day long and walk hand in hand with the Lord through the communion of the Holy Spirit.

Once conversational praying is functional in our lives, the feedback from the Lord will flow back to the individual. No one can say how the Lord will solve a problem on a day. We depend on Him always to steer our path away from sin and evil to godliness.

Through conversational praying, we learn when to run away from certain situations. We also learn when not to engage at all rather than engage and be struggling to be disentangled. Obedience will always lead us to victory, for the LORD knows the way through the wilderness that is life in this world.

The Lord may lead us to seek godly counsel in certain situations. We always remember that 'no man is an island.' We need each other in this journey of life for support and counsel. But we should avoid seeking counsel to 'escape' clear instructions received during conversational praying. Yes, we can seek clarification to gain insight and a better understanding. But never seek counsel to dodge a demand by the Lord or drown out the persisting voice of the Holy Spirit within. Such a move always sets us back spiritually.

No man can predict how the Lord will solve a problem in another person's life except by the exercise of the gift of the Holy Ghost.

It is not unusual for people to come to a man in whom the Spirit of the Lord is in operation and have the solution given them and their private communion confirmed. But because of the demands of the solution, some still refuse to obey. Instead, you will often hear that they have been fasting and praying for days for the Lord to deliver them from their problem.

I consider such exercise of fasting and prayer useless, especially after the Lord has told you what to do, and you have refused to do it. Fasting will not bribe God; neither will gifts and sacrifices.

"And Samuel said, Hath the Lord as great delight in burnt offerings and sacrifices [you may insert your own bribe to God—fasting, praying, religious zeal and other activity, active church membership, caring for the needs of the poor, and the pastors of God, etcetera] as in obeying the voice of the Lord? Behold, to obey is better than [insert all your good work bribes] sacrifice and to hearken than the fat of rams [all your gift and offering bribes.]

"For rebellion [i. e., when you refuse to do what the Lord has asked you to do,] is as the sin of witchcraft, and stubbornness [i. e., when you insist on doing it your own way instead of doing what the Lord has asked you to do] is as iniquity and idolatry. Because thou hast rejected the word of the Lord [i. e., the thing God has asked you to do] He has also rejected thee from being king [i.e., you cannot wield the anointing of the Lord as His king or priest].

—1 Samuel 15:22-23

See also Revelation 1:5-6, where we are made kings and priests unto God our Father through Christ.

Some try to play tricks. In their conversational praying, God would have told them what to do. But then they begin to rationalize. "How am I sure it is God?" Let us take this question to the next chapter.

CHAPTER SIX

CONVERSATIONAL PRAYER — THE BASIS FOR A CHRISTIAN'S SUCCESS

I believe that one of the fascinating studies a Christian can ever undertake in his life is the study of the man called Jesus. Let us see how the blind man in John chapter 9 saw it:

"The neighbors, therefore, and they which before had seen him that he was blind, said. Is not this he that sat and begged?

"Some said; This is he: Others said, He is like him: but he said, I am he:

"Therefore, said they unto him. How were your eyes opened?

"He answered and said, A MAN THAT IS CALLED JESUS made clay, anointed my eyes, and said unto me. Go to the Pool of Siloam, and wash: and I went and washed, and I received sight.

"Then said they unto him, 'Where is He?' He said I know not.

— John 9:8-12

This gentleman was unrecognizable after a man called Jesus touched him. Those who knew him before could not recognize him anymore. He was now totally different because a man named Jesus touched him.

Our Lord Jesus waited for thirty years to begin a ministry He was fully aware of by the age of twelve:

"And when He was twelve years old, they went up to Jerusalem after the custom of the feast.

"And when they had fulfilled the days, as they returned, the child Jesus tarried behind in Jerusalem; and Joseph and His mother knew not of it.

"But they, supposing Him to have been in the company, went a day's journey; and they sought Him among their kinsfolk and acquaintance.

"And when they found Him not, they turned back again to Jerusalem, seeking Him.

"And it came to pass, that after three days, they found Him in the temple, sitting amid the doctors, both hearing them, and asking them questions.

"And all that heard Him were astonished at His understanding and answers.

"And when they saw Him, they were amazed: and His mother said unto Him, Son, why hast thou thus dealt with us? Behold thy father, and I have sought thee sorrowing.

"And He said unto them, How is it that ye sought me? Wist ye not that I must be about my Father's business?

"And they understood not the saying which He spake unto them.

"And He went down with them and came to Nazareth and was subject unto them: but His mother kept all these sayings in her heart.

"And Jesus increased in wisdom and stature, and in favor with God and man.

—Luke 2:42-52

The impression we get here is of a boy who was somewhat in a hurry to begin the work that was boiling in His heart. He knew what His Father sent Him to do. He had a full grasp of it. He saw very clearly on His first exposure that the society in which He lived needed His message desperately. There was so much misrepresentation of His Father in the current day's theological debate that He felt compelled to begin the correction of the established wrong notions and perceptions of God.

His parents were unaware of this zeal and burden. Their paternal and maternal protective instincts were uppermost in their minds. "After all this is only our little boy of yesterday. He can't be that independent-minded already."

But the Bible records that Mary, His mother, was consistently aware of her son's uniqueness.

But in verse 51, we see our Lord Jesus, as it were, being cautioned by the Holy Ghost not to jump the gun like Moses tried to do. (Exodus 2:11-15).

The Bible records in Luke 2:51 that after this premature exposure, He withdrew to Nazareth to attend to routine family chores, waiting for the Holy Ghost's signal to commence the work.

Again, in John 2:1-4, we are given an impressive insight into the sacredness of waiting for God's fullness of time.

"And the third day there was a marriage in Cana of Galilee: and the mother of Jesus was there:

"And both Jesus was called, and His disciples, to the marriage.

"And when they wanted wine, the mother of Jesus saith unto Him they have no wine.

"Jesus saith unto her, Woman, what have I to do with thee? Mine hour is not yet come.

One of the by-products of conversational prayer is determining with the Holy Spirit when the time has fully come, or what we may prefer to call, God's fullness of time. Conversational prayer or talking things over with our guide, the Holy Spirit, helps us not jump the gun and be disqualified, or worse still, side-tracked completely. If one is disqualified, he may have to await another opportunity. But if he is side-tracked, then he is off the path entirely. Grace will often offer a fresh opportunity to a disqualified candidate who tried to jump the gun as we see clearly in Scriptures, in the life of Moses.

But there were kings like Saul and Solomon who got side-tracked and lost out in the end.

We do not begin to appreciate the place of conversational prayer and obtaining decisions from the Lord until we look closely at the man called Jesus.

The deep impression that our Lord Jesus left behind, particularly as we study the Gospel of John closely, is that He is none other than a simple conduit for the perfect will of God in every situation.

Listen to Him speak about it:

"Jesus saith unto them, My meat is to do the will of Him that sent me, and to finish His work."

—John 4:34

"But Jesus answered them, My Father worketh hitherto and I work."

—John 5:17

"Then answered Jesus and said unto them, verily, verily, I say unto you, the Son can do nothing of himself, but what He seeth the Father do: For what things soever He doeth, these also doeth the son likewise.

"For the Father loveth the Son, and sheweth Him all things that himself doeth: and He will show Him greater works than these, that ye may marvel.

"For as the Father raiseth up the dead, and quickeneth them; even so the Son quickeneth whom He will."

—John 5:18-21

"I can of mine own self do nothing: as I hear, I judge and my judgement is just, because I seek not mine own will, but the will of the Father which hath sent Me."

—John 5:30

"Jesus answered them, and said, My doctrine is not mine, but His that sent Me.

"If any man will do His will, he shall know of the doctrine, whether it be of God, or whether I speak of Myself.

"He that speaketh of himself seeketh his own glory. But he that seeketh his glory that sent Him, the same is true, and no unrighteousness is in Him."

—John 7:16-18

"Then cried Jesus in the temple as He taught, saying ye both know me, and ye know whence I am: and I am not come of Myself, but He that sent me is true, whom ye know not.

"But I know Him: for I am from Him, and He hath sent Me."

—John 7:28-29

"Jesus cried and said, He that believeth on Me believeth not on Me, but on Him that sent Me.

"And he that seeth Me seeth Him that sent Me.

"I am come a light into the world, that whosoever believeth on Me should not abide in darkness.

"And if any man hear My words, and believe not, I judge him not: for I came not to judge the world, but to save the world.

"He that rejecteth Me, and receiveth not My words, hath one that judgeth him: the word that I have spoken, the same shall judge him in the last day.

"For I have not spoken of myself; but the Father who sent Me, He gave Me a commandment, what I should say, and what I should speak.

"And I know that His commandment is life everlasting: whatsoever I speak therefore, even as the Father said unto Me, so I speak."

—John 12:44-50

"He went away again the second time, and prayed, saying O my Father, if this cup may not pass away from me, except I drink it, thy will be done."

—Matthew 26:42

Having gone through these declarations and affirmations, you may have noticed the manner of prayer in the last quoted passage in Matt. 26:42. It is purely conversational. It addresses the issue in a kind of discussion with the Father.

In Matthew 26:39, we read: "And He went a little further, and fell on His face, and prayed [talked to God simply] saying, O my Father, if it be possible, let this cup pass from Me: nevertheless, not as I will, but as thou wilt."

It is most interesting to study the content and pattern of these two simple prayers. As we study them more closely, we come away with the definite impression that there was undoubtedly feedback between the first prayer in verse 39 and the second prayer in verse 42.

If we stretch our meditation slightly further, we see our Lord Jesus clearly in conversation with the Father. He goes before God and says, "Lord, if it is possible, let's find another way to solve the problem of the sin of man, and his reconciliation with You. But Lord, please note that I am committed to doing it exactly Your way."

Then there comes the interval when He goes to inspect His co-prayer warriors how they were doing. When He saw them sleeping, He was hurt. He addressed His hurt to the leader of the group. "Peter, could you not watch with Me one hour?" Then He returns, and we notice that the prayer has changed slightly.

It would appear that while on His visit to His disciples to see what they were doing, the Lord had said to Him in love: "Son, but you know that there is no other way. We had agreed on this in the beginning. The Cross is the only way to return our creation to fellowship with us again."

After hearing that kind of loving discourse, Jesus now returns to His prayer tower and says to His Father, "Lord, if that is the way it must be, then so let it be as You will." Amen.

CONVERSATIONAL PRAYER AND DECISION MAKING (CHOOSING OF THE DISCIPLES) — MARK 1:35

Having understood the approach to conversational prayer, let us take time to look in detail at how our Lord Jesus practiced it. Before I understood the manner of conversational prayer, I had always wondered what our Lord Jesus said to God during His reported all-night prayer meetings with the Lord. Even after I started to pray in other tongues, I realized that often I could pray for a long time, mainly when there was a burden, but when there was no burden, I couldn't sustain such an effort for very long.

Take the choice of the twelve disciples for an example. It is the account in St. Luke's Gospel that brings out the details of the antecedent preparation.

"And it came to pass in those days, that He went out into a mountain to pray, and continued all night in prayer to God.

"And when it was day, He called unto Him His disciples, and of them, He chose twelve, whom also He named Apostles.

—Luke 6:12-13

The account in St. Mark's Gospel reveals the purpose of singling out twelve people out of the many who followed Him.

"And He goeth up into a mountain, and calleth unto Him whom He would, and they came unto Him.

"And He ordained twelve, that they should be with Him, and that He might send them forth to preach, and to have the power to heal sicknesses and to cast out demons."

—Mark 3:13-15

As we look at this passage very closely, we immediately can see some kind of parallel with the advice Jethro gave to his son-in-law Moses in Exodus 18:13-26:

"And it came to pass on the morrow, that Moses sat to judge the people: and the people stood by the morning unto the evening.

"And when Moses' father-in-law saw all that he did to the people, he said, 'what is this thing that thou doest to the people? Why sittest thou thyself alone, and all the people stand by thee from morning unto even?'"

"And Moses said unto his father-in-law 'Because the people come unto me to enquire of God:

'When they have a matter, they come unto me; and I judge between one and another, and I do make them know the statutes of God, and His laws.'"

"And Moses' father-in-law said unto him, The thing that thou doest is not good.

"Thou wilt surely wear away, both thou, and this people that is with thee: for this thing is too heavy for thee; thou art not able to perform it thyself alone.

"Hearken now unto my voice, I will give thee counsel, and God shall be with thee: Be thou for the people to God-ward, that thou mayest bring the causes unto God:

"And thou shall teach them ordinances and laws, and shalt show them the way wherein they must walk, and the work that they must do.

"Moreover thou shalt provide out of all people able men, such as fear God, men of truth, hating covetousness; and place such over them, to be rulers of thousands, and rulers of hundreds, rulers of fifties, and rulers of tens:

"And let them judge the people at all seasons: and it shall be, that every great matter they shall bring unto thee, but every small matter they shall judge: so shall it be easier for thyself, and they shall bear the burden with thee.

"If thou shall do this thing, and God command thee so, then thou shalt be able to endure, and all these people shall also go to their place in peace.

"So, Moses hearkened to the voice of the father-in-law and did all that he had said.

"And Moses chose able men out of all Israel and made them heads over the people, rulers of thousands, rulers of hundreds, rulers of fifties, and rulers of tens.

"And they judged the people at all seasons, the hard causes they brought unto Moses, but every small matter they judged themselves."

This advice is what we may call wise counsel. Moses' father-in-law, however, did urge Moses to ensure that God also commands it. He did not say do it. He said it is a good thing to do. You may find out from God.

Our Lord Jesus Christ demonstrated a firm grasp of the Scriptures. He always urged his Jewish listeners to search the Scriptures (John 5:39).

He must have read the two accounts of the delegation of authority concerning Moses's leadership role.

When we compare the two accounts, we immediately notice a significant difference:

"I am not able to bear all these people alone because it is too heavy for me. ..

"And the Lord said unto Moses, Gather unto me seventy men of the elders of Israel, whom thou knowest to be the elders of the people, and officers over them; and bring them unto the tabernacle of the congregation, that they may stand there with thee.

"And I will come down and talk with thee there: and I will take of the spirit which is upon thee, and will put it upon them, and they shall bear the burden of the people with thee, that thou bear it not thyself alone.

"And the Lord came down in a cloud, and spake unto him, and took of the spirit that was upon him, and gave it unto the seventy elders: and it came to pass, that when the spirit rested upon them, they prophesied and did not cease.

"But there remained two of the men in the camp, the name of the one was Eldad, and the name of the other Medad: and the spirit rested upon them; and they were of them that were written, but went not out unto the tabernacle: and they prophesied in the camp.

"And there ran a young man, and told Moses and said, Eldad and Medad do prophesy in the camp.

"And Joshua, the son of Nun, the servant of Moses, one of his young men, answered and said. My Lord Moses forbid them.

"And Moses said unto him, "Enviest thou for my sake?

"Would God that all the Lord's people were prophets,

and that the Lord would put His spirit upon them.

—Numbers 11:14, 16-17, 24-29

The most significant point to emerge out of the comparison of these two passages is the criterion for choice.

Jethro, Moses' father-in-law, urged him to choose able men of integrity. But God added that these men should also be elders of the people who naturally would be more readily acceptable to the people.

Again, Jethro's advice did not suggest any fixed numbers, but the Lord pegged the number at seventy.

Delegation of authority also had its problems. The center of power may lose some of its aura by authority delegation, and the leader may lose part of his overshadowing influence. As a young disciple under Moses, Joshua was quick to notice the immediate impact of authority delegation to reduce Moses's power base when Medad and Eldad started to prophesy in the camp.

But Moses showed impressive spiritual maturity, revealing that the work God has called him to do was much more significant than his person, and so the work must come first.

Our Lord Jesus Christ was a great student of the Bible as it then was. He faced the burden of an ever expanding ministry. I could see

Him pick up His Bible and head for the mountains to discuss the matter with God alone.

He must have taken time to review these accounts of Moses as He sat there before His Father. He must have noted the various ways that Moses used to arrive at the number seventy.

I could sense the Lord ask Him to choose some close companions whom He should teach in detail and then use as the springboard for the continuation of His ministry.

But you may wonder, "How can that last all night?" But when we consider that our Lord Jesus had thousands of followers, then we can imagine that He must have taken time to discuss each of them with the Father.

It is not too difficult to imagine a conversation like this in that all-night prayer meeting: "Father, what do you think about Simon?"

And the Lord will reply, "Yes, Simon should be there, and You should put him in charge."

Then it may have continued this way: "Father, remember that Simon has this quality of being unsteady. Isn't that a great flaw in a leader?"

"Yes, I agree, Son. But you know, Simon has energy and zeal, and he is straightforward, too. He is quick to embrace truth and also quick to admit errors. That is something you need in a leader. We can work on his instability, and that will improve."

We could easily have heard our Lord Jesus say: "Father, but what about John? He is sensitive, too, and is deep. He listens so attentively and appears not to be too easily carried away by events. He notes teaching details much better than the rest and might serve as a more qualified leader than Simon."

Then the Father would reply, "Yes, I agree with You there, Son. John is deep. Yes, certainly. But John is not a firebrand. This work at this stage requires a firebrand personality to lead it. What you can do is to make Simon, John, and his brother, James, your inner circle. John's depth will compensate for Simon's simple mindedness. But Simon should still be in charge. I will soon make him stand out among the rest, so they can accept his leadership" (see Matthew 16:13—20).

At the end of a conversation like this, I could see our Lord Jesus noting the names of Peter, James, and John down in His little notebook.

Let us imagine the conversation about people like Thomas and Judas Iscariot.

Remember, the Bible told us that our Lord Jesus knew all men (John 2:24). So He comes before God with an all-embracing knowledge of each of His disciples.

For Thomas, I could imagine the Father saying to our Lord Jesus, "Son, add Thomas to that list."

And our Lord Jesus would have said, "Father, You know Thomas. He listens attentively, but he doesn't stir except he sees a demonstration. During the teaching sessions, he pays attention, but he always wears this look of disbelief."

And the Father would have said, "Son, put him anyway. He will prove a great asset in the end."

Now comes the conversation on Judas Iscariot. I could hear the Father say something like this to His Son, Jesus. "Son, do you know Judas has to be there?"

"Father, does he have to be? You know Judas. He doesn't really belong here. He is an opportunist. He is looking for money, fame, and power. You are sure you really want him as one of my closest companions?"

"You know why he has to be there. Son? I don't have to go into too many details. You recall what I said when Lucifer deceived Adam and Eve?"

"Yes, I remember. It is this question of bruising of his head and bruising of my heels" (Genesis 3:15).

"Yes, Son. Judas is part of that program. So just put him there. There is no one else on that list that has the potential to cooperate with the devil. He is vulnerable because he lusts for power, money, and fame."

"But, Father, if he joins the group, I will work hard on him to change that part of him. I will entrust him with special responsibilities to steer him away from Lucifer."

"Well, Son, I would love to see you try. But these feelings in him run very deep. I don't think he will respond. But you are right there, Son. Give him all the opportunity to grow and resist Lucifer. If he does, then we will do it another way."

It is not too difficult to see how a prayer meeting like this can last all night. At the end of it, one comes out, not tired but refreshed.

No wonder early the next morning, our Lord Jesus descended from the mountain, called the multitude of His disciples together, and named twelve Apostles.

You can imagine the reaction of some among the crowd as He called the list.

Some would say: "I expect Peter, James and John and Andrew to be there, after all, James and John are His cousins, and Peter and Andrew were with them at Galilee as fishermen. So he is calling those who can work together." Some in the crowd would have expected to hear their names. Some would have been disappointed. The list was made up by God the Father, not by our Lord Jesus (John 17:6, Matthew 20:20-23).

When our Lord named Judas as one of the group there may have been some who knew him who would have been offended and ask, "That fellow is not serious. How can He name him?

God always has His reasons.

As we review the whole scenario, we can see that conversational prayer derives from two primary sources: Meditation on God's word that relates to the issue in question; and conversation with God in detail concerning the subject.

Let us take a further look at that list of the Lord's early disciples. We note that our Lord Jesus had three tiers of close associates. First, there was the innermost caucus of the three—Peter, James, and John. Then there were the twelve Apostles in council.

But the most interesting observation is that after the twelve, He chose seventy, again borrowing, as it were, from Moses, the God-directed choice of seventy elders as revealed in Luke chapter 10, verses:1, and 17.

ANOTHER PRAYER MEETING REVIEWED

Our Lord Jesus Christ had a habit of prayer. It would appear that for Him, prayer was strategy time, the time to discuss plans and details with His Father.

The Gospel of Mark opened with a staccato of miracles. The first chapter noted in breathtaking detail the explosive Capernaum campaign with its strings of healing miracles, beginning at the synagogue, where He taught with authority and cast out the unclean spirit. His fame spread everywhere (Mark 1:28).

He left the synagogue for Simon's house, and there He rebuked a fever.

Later that evening, He was besieged by the whole city bringing all kinds of sicknesses, diseases, and demonic possessions needing the powerful touch of the Master. Mark 1:34 summarized it all beautifully:

"And He healed many that were sick of divers diseases, and cast out many devils: and suffered not the devils to speak because they knew Him."

At the end of such a long day, our Lord Jesus being sensitive to the mind of God, thought it was time to review the results and ensure that the Father God did not intend any changes: "And in the morning, rising up a great while before day. He went out, and departed into a solitary place, and there prayed" (Mark 1:35).

Let us see if we can attend that prayer conversation and learn something more about conversational prayer. First of all, it will be a kind of report, detailing what the Holy Ghost did through Him all through the previous day.

He would be checking whether the teachings were in complete consonance with the mind of God (John 14:10).

We can begin to appreciate this better when we compare the three voices from heaven. The first voice was at the baptism of our Lord Jesus. All the synoptic gospels of Matthew, Mark, and Luke recorded it thus: "This is my beloved son in whom I am well pleased" (Mark 1:11, Matthew 3:17, Luke 3:22)

But midway into His ministry at the Mount of Transfiguration, the voice came again. This time it was not only to the effect that this is my beloved Son, in whom I am well pleased, but the voice told us to listen closely and attend to every word He says. (Matthew 17:5, Mark 9:7, Luke 9:35).

It is evident that God the Father was satisfied with the way our Lord Jesus was handling His commission, and this is why this second voice added the matter of His authority to teach and reveal the mind of God.

But let us return to this second prayer meeting. Besides the report, there was also the strategy session.

We begin to gain insight into that in His encounter with His disciples after this prayer meeting:

"And Simon and they that were with Him followed after Him.

"And when they had found Him, they said unto Him, All men seek thee.

"And He said unto them. Let us go into the next towns that I may preach there also: For therefore came I forth.

"And He preached in the synagogues throughout all Galilee and cast out devils.

—Mark 1:35-39

We can see the result of the strategic planning session here. The disciples met Him with a report that the whole city was looking for Him. Our Lord's reply must have been a bit disappointing to them. He said, "Sorry, we are moving on. We are not going back there."

This decisive switch must have come from the strategy session's details during the prayer conference with God the Father.

As ministers of the great truth of the Lord God, it behooves us all to follow the pattern of our Lord and hold regular strategy planning sessions with God so He can give us detailed and precise directives.

THE PUBLIC PRAYERS OF JESUS

Conversational prayer appears to be the only way to have a meaningful relationship with God. In the three public prayers of our Lord Jesus, recorded for us in the Bible, we note that all of them were conversational. They reflected the reality of the deep and personal relationship that our Lord Jesus Christ had with His Father.

THE RAISING OF LAZARUS FROM DEATH

The story of Lazarus's death and rising from death will be quite familiar to most readers of this book (John 11:1-45).

Our Lord Jesus arrived at the graveside of Lazarus four days after his death and burial. He stood there mourning His friend and lamenting the wickedness of the agents of death in snuffing out the life of a young man. He prayed to His Father:

"And Jesus lifted up His eyes and said, 'Father, I thank thee that thou hast heard Me.

'And I knew that thou hearest Me always. But because of the people which standby I said it, that they might believe that thou hast sent Me.'

"And when He thus had spoken, He cried with a loud voice, 'Lazarus, come forth.' And he that was dead came forth."

—John 11:41-44

As we look at this prayer closely, it would appear that our Lord Jesus had held an earlier conversation with His Father about the impending miracle of raising the dead before reaching the graveside of Lazarus. As a result of that conversation and the assurances, He received, He prayed publicly: "Father, I thank thee that thou hast heard me."

Then the second sentence was more or less to reassure His Father that this public prayer did not in any way reflect unbelief, "And I know that thou hearest me always."

He proceeded in the third sentence to tell His Father why He thought it necessary that He should make what would appear to be an unnecessary public prayer. "But because of the people which stand by I said it, that they might believe that thou hast sent Me."

This public prayer of Jesus was just to assist the onlookers to develop their faith in Him. By speaking to God, they will appreciate the source of His power and that He is none other than the Son of God.

HIS PRAYER OF INTERCESSION FOR THE CHURCH —JOHN 17:1-26

Let me state that the objective here is not to study this prayer. We are looking at the conversational way in which He prayed: A way that reflects deep intimacy and knowledge of God the Father.

It behooves each of us to study the prayer style revealed here and draw close to God as one would an earthly father, and talk to Him.

A brief panoramic view reveals that here we have a report of the whole program or His mission to the world at the close of it. "I have glorified thee on the earth: I have finished the work which thou gavest me to do" (John 17:4).

Having made the report, He dwelt considerably on continuity. He told His Father about the men that He, God the Father, chose to continue the work:

"I have manifested thy name unto the men which thou gavest me out of the world: thine they were, thou gavest them to me; and they have kept thy word" (John 17:6).

What follows is His prayer requests on behalf of the men who were to continue the work. As we dwell more and more on this, we see His concerns coming forth the way He felt them. "I pray not that thou shouldst take them out of the world, but that thou shouldst keep them from evil" (John 17:15).

It is not unusual for many of us to speak to God in prayer and fail to open our hearts to God and talk with Him freely and honestly. This example of our Lord Jesus should teach us that, indeed, anyone who can speak can pray.

Therefore, a good prayer would be a conversational one that reflects the degree of intimacy one has with the LORD God Almighty.

We need to remember that meditating on God's word helps us learn how to talk simply to God. It is God's word that reveals God's mind and ways and assists us to converse with Him aright.

THE PRAYER AT GETHSEMANE (LUKE 22:40–46)

This is the third recorded prayer of our Lord Jesus. As He prayed in Gethsemane about the ordeal of the Cross, we notice that His words were few and direct to the point (Matthew 6:7).

St. Luke recorded that God the Father, sent an angel to our Lord Jesus to strengthen Him and commune with Him. He was in deep agony of soul, but He spoke only a few words.

Talking with God and hearing God speak to us is the cornerstone of a meaningful, impactful, and the victorious

Christian life.

CHAPTER SEVEN

STRATEGIES IN PRAYER

I would love to give some credit to the message that gave birth to this book as much as possible. That message dealt with what I called strategies in prayer. These are the principles in God's word that help us know how to pray with our understanding.

To put this in perspective, I would like to discuss a few of these to highlight the fact that some prayers are ineffective because the strategies are wrong. Let us begin with nations.

PRAYING FOR THE NATION

To appreciate how the Lord would have us pray for a nation, we would need to see how prayer radically impacted the life of nations in the Word of God.

Let us take the children of Israel, for instance. We will try to see the pathway they took in emerging as a nation. Perhaps this will assist us in seeing the finger of God in the life of a nation.

THE PROMISE

Now the Lord had said unto Abram, Get thee out of thy country, and from thy kindred, and from thy father's house, unto a land that I will show thee.

And I will make of thee a great Nation, and I will bless thee and make thy name great, and thou shall be a blessing.

And I will bless them that bless thee, and curse him that curseth thee: and in thee shall all families of the earth be blessed.

—Genesis 12:1-3

Abram responded to this promise and moved from Syria to Canaan or present-day Israel. Significantly, Abram was childless at this stage, yet he received and held onto this blessing.

THE MAKING OF A NATION

In Genesis 15, the Lord renewed this promise to Abram. In Genesis 15:6, the Bible records that Abram believed in the Lord, and He counted it to him for righteousness.

Verse thirteen pointed the way to the birth process of this nation.

And He said unto Abram, Know of a surety that thy seed shall be a stranger in the land that is not theirs, and shall serve them, and they shall afflict them four hundred years.

And also that nation whom they shall serve, will I judge: and afterward shall they come out with great substance.

—Genesis 15:13-14

At the threshold of this nation's birth, God sketched four hundred years of history before their founding father.

If we follow the story closely, the circumstances that brought this about were the seven years of famine worldwide in the days of Jacob, the grandson of Abraham. Joseph ascended to the throne of Egypt next only to Pharaoh and then compelled his people to come to Egypt to live to escape the famine's ravages (Genesis 42:46).

This move to Egypt started not as slavery, but just as a mere escape from famine in Canaan, taking advantage of Joseph's position in Egypt's ruling circles.

THE MAKING OF A NATION PROPER

It is interesting to watch the unfolding of this history. It gives us great insight into the ways of God and how we ought to pray for our nation (Exodus 1:8):

"Now there arose up a new king over Egypt, which knew not Joseph.

"And he said unto his people, Behold, the people of the children of Israel are more and mightier than we:

"Come on, let us deal wisely with them; lest they multiply, and it come to pass, that, when there falleth out any war, they also join unto our enemies, and fight against us, and so get them up out of the land.

"Therefore, they did set over them taskmasters to afflict them with their burdens. And they built for Pharaoh treasure cities, Pithom and Raamses.

"But the more they afflicted them, the more they multiplied and grew. And they were grieved because of the children of Israel.

"And the Egyptians made the children of Israel to serve with rigour:

"And they made their lives bitter, with hard bondage, in mortar, and in brick, and in all manner of service in the field: all their service, wherein they made them serve, was with rigour.

—Exodus 1:8-14

At a cursory glance, one may lose the significance of this chapter of the story in their nation's evolution. In retrospect, we can see the importance of having these people work as slaves in the most advanced country on earth. As slaves, they acquired skills as architects, engineers, craftsmen, artisans, joiners, carpenters, weavers, et cetera. They developed these skills working for the Egyptians. But it was these same skills they required to build their nation when the opportunity came.

So far, in this nation's history, we see the divine purpose, working out under strange and often unpleasant circumstances. But the fact remained that this period of stagnation and slavery was, in fact, the most critical phase in their development as a nation. The people themselves did not see it at the time. They could only see the humiliation and rigors of their slave labor.

One day, however, God felt that they were ready to go. They had acquired enough skills to stand on their own feet.

The exciting thing is, how did God go about this? How did he achieve this Herculean task?

GOD'S DELIVERER EMERGES

A comical Christian poster reads: "God so loved the world, that He did not send a committee."

Undoubtedly, if God had appointed a committee among the slaves to organize their exodus from Egypt, the committee would have come up with a thousand and one reasons why such a project amounted to nothing but suicide. They would explain in a thousand and one ways why they thought the plan was logistically unfeasible.

If a committee were handling the project, they would have formed more committees. For example, we would have heard of the transportation committee to cater to the aged and the young, the food committee to see to the provisions, and the armed forces committee to plan for possible wars.

But what did the Lord do? He chose a man. He got His man into the family of Pharaoh through the back door to give him a royal education and make him royal and well acquainted with the ways of the court of Pharaoh.

At the fullness of time, He made Moses fully aware that he was to lead Israel's budding nation out of bondage from Egypt.

But how was Moses to do it? Moses had his idea of what he should be doing.

"And it came to pass in those days, when Moses was grown, that he went out unto his brethren, and looked on their burdens: and he spied an Egyptian smiting a Hebrew, one of his brethren.

"And he looked this way and that way, and when he saw that there was no man, he slew the Egyptian, and hid him in the sand.

—Exodus 3:11-12

But God was to reveal to him several years later that He had His plans to accomplish the task. By closely following God's detailed instructions, Moses achieved the seemingly impossible task of leading three million people out of Egypt in one day.

Sometimes when we pray for our nation, we are carried away by particular problems that we see in the country. It may be crimes, corruption or the economy, or the educational system, et cetera. We may have our pet concerns about the nation. But the most important thing that we learn is that God's solution to any nation's problem is to provide the right kind of leader that they need.

Once this leader emerges, he would have God's wisdom to know how to solve the intricate problems that confront the nation.

The leader will always be committed to the nation's survival, just like Moses was committed. The survival of the country will become for that individual a consuming passion.

Prayers will move God to let that leader emerge. Once the people continue to intercede for God to intervene in their body politic, that leader will emerge. Once he appears, the nation will move forward in a definite and purposeful direction. He will render justice with wisdom and integrity and cause the country to prosper under his rule.

Moses was a leader who led the children of Israel out of bondage to God. It was not from bondage to freedom alone, but from bondage to God.

As Christians in any nation pray for their country, they should ask the Lord to send the men and women chosen by Him to lead them out of social, economic, and spiritual slavery to their land of promise.

This approach is following God's wonderful and universal promise to His people in any nation: "If my people, which are called by my name, shall humble themselves, and pray, and seek my face, and turn from their wicked ways; then will I hear from heaven, and will forgive their sin, and will heal their land" (2 Chron. 7:14).

As men and women with the fear of God in their hearts, as men and women guided by the Holy Spirit appear in various leadership positions, they will discuss the multi-faceted problems of their nation with the Holy Ghost conversationally. As they receive advice from technocrats and professionals, they will allow the Holy Spirit to determine their country's pathway amid the clamor and din of competing interests. The outcome will be that their nation will move slowly but steadily towards the goal of comprehensive stability and prosperity— socially, economically, and spiritually, as was witnessed in Israel in the days of Kings David and Solomon, his son.

Someone has said, and I agree that there is enough in the world for everybody's needs but not for everybody's greed. Only through God's wisdom can we bring some order into human society—order with love and humaneness.

PRAYING FOR PERSONAL NEEDS

Conversational Prayer becomes most useful when one is confronted with personal needs, no matter what the need may be. We have this authorization Scripture that says:

"And this is the confidence that we have in Him, that, if we ask anything according to His will, He heareth us:

"And if we know that He hear us, whatsoever we ask, we know that we have the petitions that we desired of Him."

—1 John 5:14-15

What we see in the Bible is that the promises of God are universal in their application, but only in a general sort of way. Each particular blessing still has to be appropriated by the individual.

Let us take a universal promise like this: "But my God shall supply all your need according to His riches in glory by Christ Jesus." (Philippians 4:19).

This promise covers every and any need conceivable, but only in a universal sort of way.

However, an individual still has to determine the place of each particular need in God's overall purpose for his or her life, at the material time of asking, so that he or she may place the request in its correct perspective.

In the light of this thinking, we might reconstruct that passage in 1 John 5:14-15 to read something like this:

"And this is the confidence that we have in Him, that if we ask anything according to His will (*in general, and in particular*), He hears us:

"And if we know that He hear us, whatsoever we ask, we know that we have the petitions that we desire of Him.

It is this aspect of prayer for personal needs that compelled the apostle and elder James to write: "Ye lust, and have not: ye kill and desire to have, and cannot obtain: ye fight and war, yet ye have not because ye ask not. Ye ask, and receive not, because ye ask amiss, that ye may consume it upon your lusts" (James 4:2-3).

The above passage implies that a universal promise that says: "Ask, and ye shall receive" (Luke 11:9) may be grounded in an individual's particular experience at a specific time because of certain spiritual immaturity that he is exhibiting in the related area or areas.

So whereas the promise is universal and can be obtained by faith: "Therefore I say unto you, what things soever ye desire, when ye pray, believe that ye receive them, and ye shall have them" (Mark 11:24), an individual may have obstacles in the particular which pose a significant hindrance.

MOVING TO RECEIVE YOUR NEEDS

When confronted with this kind of situation, an individual may do some things:

Believe that demonic obstacles are obstructing his blessings and so proceed to bind and loosen powers against and for him.

Believe that he has not prayed hard enough, and so embark on prayer and fasting with much interceding in the spirit.

Believe that he has not got enough faith, so go out searching for an anointed preacher to pray for him and minister to him.

Worse still, he may seek other powers, often disguised as Christian, because of the pressure of his needs. One can easily recognize these powers by their emphasis. They will prescribe specific rituals, types of prayers, candles, and a specific number of days of fasting.

Indeed, all things put together it may be that one has not prayed enough, and the delay on that particular occasion may only be God's way of saying, "Son, you'd better grow up and come closer."

LACK OF FAITH

This deficit may be so in a particular situation. When the disciples wondered why they could not exorcise the demon spirit in the epileptic boy at the foot of the Mount of Transfiguration (Matthew 17:19-21), our Lord Jesus took time to point out to them that their inability was primarily due to unbelief. He also prescribed there the cure for the lack of power—praying and fasting.

THE PLACE OF PRAYER AND FASTING

Many have allowed this prescription to degenerate into an ungodly ritual. It has reached an extent in some lives where expectations are dependent on the degree of preparation in fasting and praying rather than on the Holy Ghost's anointing. This attitude is a subtle dependence on works, sometimes so subtle that it fools the unwary.

Fasting and prayer can only be effective if we use the period to build our faith in God and His Word. It is during this period that we build intimacy with the Lord and feel His presence and anointing envelop us.

During this period, we receive precise instructions as to what we should do so that God's kingdom on earth can move forward as it relates to us (1 Kings 19:1-21).

Fasting is not a ritual; neither is it a bribe to God. Fasting is a religious observance that is common to virtually every religion under the sun. Fasting can be started in total ignorance of the true God and His Son and ended the same way. It is a mere religious observance. Again, fasting even for believers can begin in unbelief and end in unbelief.

The Scriptures do not say that "prayer under fasting will save the sick." It says, "the prayer of faith will save the sick."

If fasting is to meditate on God's word and build a deep faith in God in our hearts, then it is good. But if fasting is an end in itself, something to do to force God to move on our behalf, then it is a mere ritual.

SEEING OTHER POWERS

I believe I do not need to dwell a lot on this, save to point out some ways to recognize spurious sources of power. Each time we receive prescriptions of sorts from so-called spiritual leaders, detailing what and what we ought to bring or pay to have our needs met, we should always be cautious.

I prefer to consider these prescriptions as valueless short-cuts. The reason is that there is usually no consideration whatsoever whether the individual has been born again or not. There is no attempt to get them to see that they need a personal revelation of Jesus as the Lord of their lives before they can transfer their burdens to Him. These so-called spiritual houses only prescribe ways to solve problems, and usually, there is no biblical basis for these prescriptions.

It is important to mention to those who may seek these short-cut prescriptions that unknown to them, most times, their so-called spiritual leader is a medium, harnessing demonic or occult powers.

All I need to do is search the Scriptures and see if their methods are in the Bible. It is that simple. The ways of God are not short-cut rituals; they come out of more in-depth knowledge of God.

The impact of the revelation knowledge of God in a man's life is like the experience of the Hebrews in the Old Testament. The period of slavery in Egypt is a type of life in unbelief and sin. This slavery is under sin and tempting devils. (Galatians 4:3, 9).

The exodus marks the new birth and the journey to the land of faith and rest, Canaan's land. But the intervening wilderness is the school of faith where one progressively captures a deepening revelation of God.

Those who wander in the wilderness go around their lives in circles, repeating the same lessons. They never get to grow in faith and to have a personal commitment to His promised word, as Joshua and Caleb typified at the borders of Canaan. Despite their numerous experiences of God's power, the rest of the multitude did not develop a personal revelation of God, nor did they become intimate with Him.

The result is their inability to see their problems in comparison with God's incredible power that brought them out of Egypt. Instead, they were always looking at their challenges in the context of their capability.

CONVERSATIONAL PRAYER AND NEEDS REVISITED

Now, as one approaches God for a particular need in his or her life, the best way to approach a close and dear friend is to discuss the matter with him, knowing as our Lord Jesus taught us that He already knows our needs (Matthew 6:7-8). This approach helps to clear the road and reduce agony considerably.

In the ensuing conversation, the Lord Himself may speak to us concerning the need directly or by leading us to a particular passage of Scripture that will shed the light we need.

Sometimes He uses another Christian brother or sister to point the way forward, or even a gospel tract or Christian literature. But what is essential is that we become aware that this is the mind of God concerning this particular need. As we pick up and confirm this mind of God in this specific matter, we can go ahead and pray for it.

To a large extent, this approach reduces uncertainty, and the trial and error exhibited in many Christian lives today.

It is vital that one progressively develops the ability to hear God clearly in our hearts through consistent obedience of God's revealed mind in the Bible as earlier discussed (Hebrews 4:12). We do not use rational deduction to predict God's mind in a situation unless it is clearly stated in the Bible. Sometimes it may coincide with logical and analytical thinking, and sometimes it may not. But whichever way it is, conversational prayer or communion will always reveal the direction in which the Holy Spirit is pointing in a particular matter at a specific time.

It is wrong to presume that God works, in the same way, each time. Experience in the Bible speaks to the contrary. God may work the same way each time for a while. But because He is God Almighty, He may choose to work in another way on this particular occasion in an individual's life. For example, in 2 Samuel 5:17-25, the newly crowned king of Israel, David, fought two wars against the Philistines. David inquired of the Lord in verse 19, and the Lord prescribed a frontal attack on the host of the Philistines.

But in verse 22, when they attacked again, David did not presume that since the Lord had prescribed a frontal attack the first time, there was no need to ask Him again, but rather just to go ahead and attack directly.

He inquired of the Lord again what strategy to use to defeat the Philistines this time. And this time, the Lord changed the prescription, recommending an ambush (verse 23). Not only did the Lord prescribe another strategy, but He also detailed the precise timing of the onset of the assault on the camp. So it is wrong to feel so spiritual, and so begin to imagine that the mind of the Lord on issues unrevealed is routine and predictable.

One way I have learned of the Lord about God's mind and our attitude to it after we have received it clearly can be illustrated in this example that the Holy Spirit gave me during one of the teaching sessions on this subject.

Suppose you see an open door before you, and you have a need that can be met through that door. Because you must hear God before you act, you decided to ask the Lord whether you should go through that door. To your greatest surprise, and contrary to all your expectations, the Lord tells you that there is no door there, even though you can see one.

In obedience to the Lord, and against your better judgment, you turn away from that seemingly open door.

Now supposing as you continue to discuss the issue with the Lord, He says, "My child, there is your door."

The conversation may go something like this: "Lord, I see a wall before me," and the Lord replies clearly: "What I see is an open door."

Based on such a clear affirmation, we would have no alternative but to conduct a spirit-guided attack on that wall so that our open door can appear. But consider the case of a man who does not engage in conversational prayer with the Lord. He sits there, wondering endlessly what the problem is. He prays hard with fasting, commands the devil, rebukes, binds, loosens, casts down, speaks faith, and quotes Scriptures in the hope that one or two of all these approaches will hit the target and solve the problem.

This approach is no more than trial and error. Sometimes it works, because God, in His mercy and grace, recognizes our deficiencies and helps us along the way. But because what we have with Him is a dynamic relationship, sooner or later, He will expect us to approach Him first to discuss the issue or issues involved for Him to chart our pathway for us.

THE UNIVERSAL AND THE PARTICULAR IN CONVERSATIONAL PRAYER

This topic bears repeating because the devil has used confusion in this area to keep several believers in bondage. But recourse to conversational prayer will always clear the confusion.

Let us look at two clear-cut examples in the Bible.

The disciples of our Lord Jesus had issues with this distinction between the universal and the particular. In John 5:1-15, we read of the healing of the person with paralysis at the pool of Bethesda. Our Lord Jesus came upon the man said to have been paralyzed for thirty-eight years and asked him, "Would thou be made whole?" (John 5:6)

After he was made whole, our Lord saw him again in the temple and said these words in John 5:15: "... Behold, thou art made whole: sin no more, lest a worst thing come upon thee."

The disciples must have noted this strange rebuke and possibly concluded that all these chronically sick people and people with paralysis, blind and maimed, were terrible sinners.

They found an excellent example in John, chapter 9, to test their concept. They met a man who was born blind. They must have felt their theology being shaken to its foundation when they realized that this gentleman was born blind. They decided to confront our Lord Jesus with the question.

"And His disciples asked Him, saying, Master, who did sin, this man, or his parents, that he was born blind?

Jesus answered, "Neither this man sinned, nor his parents! But that the works of God should be made manifest in him."

—John 9:2-3

So, we see two clear pictures of chronically ill people who our Lord Jesus healed. One was sick because of sin; the other was sick, so God's power can be manifest in him.

Some people choose to decide which group they belong to, whether those whose sin caused their sickness or those who desire the healing power of God to be manifest in their lives. The obvious step to take, whatever the cause of the ailment, is to step forward in faith to take their healing from the broken body of Christ. He was wounded for our transgressions, and by His stripes, we are healed.

All we need to clear the confusion is a conversation with the Lord, always noting that the man who was sick due to sin and the man who was sick to manifest the power of God were both healed. They both went away healed.

CHAPTER EIGHT

SPIRITUAL EMPOWERMENT

If there is any place where we need conversational prayer the most, it is spiritual empowerment. Let us go through the promises related to the spiritual empowering of believers. First, we have the prophecy of John the Baptist in the Gospel of Matthew.

"I indeed baptize you with water unto repentance, but He who is coming after me is mightier than I, whose sandals I am not worthy to carry. He will baptize you with the Holy Spirit and fire."

—Matthew 3:11 (NKJV)

Then our Lord Jesus first announced the coming Rivers of Living Water.

"On the last day, that great *day* of the feast, Jesus stood and cried out, saying, "If anyone thirsts, let him come to Me and drink.

"He who believes in Me, as the Scripture has said, out of his heart will flow rivers of living water."

"But this He spoke concerning the Spirit, whom those believing in Him would receive; for the Holy Spirit was not yet *given,* because Jesus was not yet glorified."

—John 7:37–39 (NKJV)

And just before He departed, He asked His disciples to wait for the promise of the Father.

"Behold, I send the Promise of My Father upon you; but tarry in the city of Jerusalem until you are endued with power from on high."

—Luke 24:49 (NKJV)

And then, at His final departure, He told them that the Holy Spirit was coming to empower them for the work on hand.

"But you shall receive power when the Holy Spirit has come upon you; and you shall be witnesses to Me in Jerusalem, and in all Judea and Samaria, and to the end of the earth."

—Acts 1:8 (NKJV)

The ministry of the Holy Spirit in the Body of Christ is all-inclusive as revealed in many of our Lord's teachings:

"If you love Me, keep My commandments.

"And I will pray the Father, and He will give you another Helper, that He may abide with you forever--"the Spirit of truth, whom the world cannot receive because it neither sees Him nor knows Him; but you know Him, for He dwells with you and will be in you."

—John 14:15-17 (NKJV)

"But the Helper, the Holy Spirit, whom the Father will send in My name, He will teach you all things, and bring to your remembrance all things that I said to you."

—John 14:26 (NKJV)

"But when the Helper comes, whom I shall send to you from the Father, the Spirit of truth who proceeds from the Father, He will testify of Me."

—John 15:26 (NKJV)

"Nevertheless, I tell you the truth. It is to your advantage that I go away; for if I do not go away, the Helper will not come to you; but if I depart, I will send Him to you.

"And when He has come, He will convict the world of sin, and of righteousness, and of judgment:

"of sin, because they do not believe in Me;

"of righteousness, because I go to My Father and you see Me no more;

"of judgment, because the ruler of this world is judged.

"I still have many things to say to you, but you cannot bear *them* now.

"However, when He, the Spirit of truth, has come, He will guide you into all truth; for He will not speak on His own *authority,* but whatever He hears He will speak; and He will tell you things to come.

"He will glorify Me, for He will take of what is Mine and declare *it* to you.

"All things that the Father has are Mine. Therefore I said that He will take of Mine and declare *it* to you.

—John 16:7–15 (NKJV)

THE HOLY SPIRIT IN THE MINISTRY OF OUR LORD JESUS

We do not need to look far to see that the Holy Spirit partnered with our Lord Jesus Christ to fulfill His mission to the world. We have a summary of the lifestyle of our Lord Jesus Christ before He began His public ministry in Luke 2:52 (NKJV)

"And Jesus increased in wisdom and stature, and in favor with God and men."

At the beginning of His public ministry, we see the Holy Spirit coming down to take charge from the moment of His baptism.

"When He had been baptized, Jesus came up immediately from the water; and behold, the heavens were opened to Him, and He saw the Spirit of God descending like a dove and alighting upon Him.

"And suddenly a voice *came* from heaven, saying, "This is My beloved Son, in whom I am well pleased."

    —Matthew 3:16-17 (NKJV)

After His baptism, we see the Holy Spirit again taking charge of His program.

"Then Jesus, being filled with the Holy Spirit, returned from the Jordan and was led by the Spirit into the wilderness, "being tempted for forty days by the devil. And in those days He ate nothing, and afterward, when they had ended, He was hungry."

    —Luke 4:1-2 (NKJV)

He went through His wilderness experience where He fasted and prayed and was tempted by the devil. The devil's temptation centred on the strategy He should deploy for His mission. We learned that He emerged from the wilderness still filled with the Holy Spirit.

"Then Jesus returned in the power of the Spirit to Galilee, and news of Him went out through all the surrounding region.

"And He taught in their synagogues, being glorified by all."

    —Luke 4:14-15 (NKJV)

The Holy Spirit was central to the ministry of our Lord Jesus. He took charge of details and ensured through communion that the Father and His Son were in tandem throughout the three and half years of ministry.

YOU SHALL RECEIVE POWER

We are repeatedly told in the Scriptures that we need the Holy Spirit to function. So let us begin with John the Baptist's prophecy.

"I indeed baptize you with water unto repentance, but He who is coming after me is mightier than I, whose sandals I am not worthy to carry. He will baptize you with the Holy Spirit and fire."

—Matthew 3:11 (NKJV)

We have a twofold baptism here:

There is baptism with the Holy Spirit and baptism with fire. What is this baptism with fire? We will go to the Prophet Malachi to see a parallel prophecy.

"But who can endure the day of his coming? And who will be able to stand when he appears? For he will be like a refiner's fire and like launderer's bleach.

"He will be like a refiner and purifier of silver; he will purify the sons of Levi and refine them like gold and silver. Then they will present offerings to the Lord in righteousness."

—Malachi 3:2-3 (CSBBible)

We learn here that this is the fire of purification. It produces holiness in the lives of believers in Christ. The fire of the Holy Spirit is always for the purification of our lives.

HOW DOES THE HOLY SPIRIT PURGE US?

There must be a desire to be purged and made right with God. A man with so much pressure with righteousness can go to God in prayer to ask for faith and courage to go out on a limb as it were for righteousness' sake. The Apostle Peter added that there might be some suffering along this route of faith and holiness.

"The God of all grace, who called you to his eternal glory in Christ, will himself restore, establish, strengthen, and support you after you have suffered a little while.

"To him, be dominion forever. Amen."

   —1 Peter 5:10-11 (CSBBible)

The promise is that those who insist on getting it right with God may suffer a little because they want to be vessels of honour unto God.

"But in a great house there are not only vessels of gold and silver, but also of wood and clay, some for honor and some for dishonour.

"Therefore, if anyone cleanses himself from the latter, he will be a vessel for honour, sanctified and useful for the Master, prepared for every good work."

   —2 Timothy 2:20-21 (NKJV)

A simple prayer that says: "LORD I want to be a vessel of honour unto You. Please may Your Holy Spirit show me how to purge myself of everything that offends You to prepare my life to bring You glory daily, in Jesus name, Amen." Such a simple prayer will position us for purification that is without chastisement (Hebrews 12:5-10).

THE SPIRIT OF EMPOWERMENT

We have several promises for empowerment:

Acts 1:8: You shall receive power after the Holy Spirit has come upon you

Luke 24:49: Wait in Jerusalem until you are endued with power from on high

John 7:37-39: After the resurrection from the dead glorifies our Lord Jesus, the Holy Spirit will be released so that the thirsty can drink until they have the diversity of Rivers of Living waters flowing from within them.

WE RECEIVE BY GRACE THROUGH FAITH

We receive by grace through faith all that the LORD God Almighty has provided for us in Christ, beginning with our salvation. This is clear from the Book of Ephesians:

"For by grace you have been saved through faith, and that not of yourselves; *it is* the gift of God, "not of works, lest anyone should boast."

—Ephesians 2:8-9 (NKJV)

Grace ensures that what God provided is universally available. It also ensures that not only is it universally available but also universally accessible through faith.

"So the promise is received by faith. It is given as a free gift. And we are all certain to receive it, whether or not we live according to the law of Moses, if we have faith like Abraham's. For Abraham is the father of all who believe.

—Romans 4:16 (NLT2)

THE WAY OF FAITH

We learn the way of faith from the Bible:

"In fact, it says, "The message is very close at hand; it is on your lips and in your heart." And that message is the very message about faith that we preach:

"If you confess with your mouth that Jesus is Lord and believe in your heart that God raised him from the dead, you will be saved.

"For it is by believing in your heart that you are made right with God, and it is by confessing with your mouth that you are saved.

—Romans 10:8-10 (NLT2)

Two things are at work here.

First, there is a belief in the heart, which is consent or acceptance in the mind that whatsoever is on offer is real and authentic. After that, there is a possession through confession of what the heart has believed.

Here are the lessons we take away from this passage of Scripture:

- The way of faith is on your lips and in your heart.
- The heart is where we receive the Word and believe it as true.
- The mouth is what we use to confess what we believe in our hearts.
- As we confess what we believe in our heart to be true, just, and right, the power of God comes to actualize it as an experience. The system is simple for anyone to practice.

THE BLESSINGS PROVIDED

There is a Scripture that reveals God's promises for us who believe, particularly all the spiritual blessings He has stored for us in heavenly places as shown by Ephesians 1:3 (NLT2)

"All praise to God, the Father of our Lord Jesus Christ, who has blessed us with every spiritual blessing in the heavenly realms because we are united with Christ."

—Ephesians 1:3 (NLT2)

One of these blessings is *spiritual empowerment.* This empowerment comes to us through the indwelling presence of the Holy Spirit. The power of God is released within us and through us by the Holy Spirit that lives in us.

SPIRITUAL EMPOWERMENT

Nowhere is this revealed so well as in this passage of Scripture

"When I think of all this, I fall to my knees and pray to the Father, "the Creator of everything in heaven and on earth.

"I pray that from his glorious, unlimited resources he will empower you with inner strength through his Spirit.

"Then Christ will make his home in your hearts as you trust in him. Your roots will grow down into God's love and keep you strong.

"And may you have the power to understand, as all God's people should, how wide, how long, how high, and how deep his love is.

"May you experience the love of Christ, though it is too great to understand fully. Then you will be made complete with all the fullness of life and power that comes from God.

"Now all glory to God, who is able, through his mighty power at work within us, to accomplish infinitely more than we might ask or think.

"Glory to him in the church and in Christ Jesus through all generations forever and ever! Amen."

—Ephesians 3:14-21 (NLT2)

The strength and power we need to live as Christians in this world are deposited in our human spirit by the Spirit of God.

This power enables us to be rooted and grounded in love so that we can act like Christ our Lord in the world as revealed in 1 John 4:7-8 (NLT2)

"Dear friends, let us continue to love one another, for love comes from God. Anyone who loves is a child of God and knows God. But anyone who does not love does not know God, for God is love."

To love, like God, is to love like Christ. The love of Christ is self-sacrificing. "For God so loved the world that He gave us His Son Jesus Christ...John 3:16). For Christ so loved the world that He gave His life for all that will believe in Him as Lord and Saviour:

"This is my commandment: Love each other in the same way I have loved you. There is no greater love than to lay down one's life for one's friends."

—John 15:12-13 (NLT2)

- As we practice this self-sacrificing love in its length, breadth, depth, and height, we are transformed daily into Christ's image, and our lives will reveal the fullness of God.

- The result is that the indwelling Holy Spirit is unhindered by our soul as He expresses the life and power of God through us just the same way He did it through our Lord Jesus Christ. This liberty is why the power from within us is able to do exceedingly and abundantly above all we can ever ask or think. That power is the Holy Spirit acting with total liberty from within us as He expresses the life, the love, and the power of God through us just like He did in the life of our Lord Jesus Christ.

- This relationship with the Holy Spirit is what our Lord Jesus Christ came to model for us. He came to show how the life of God can be expressed unhindered through a human being. It is the surrender of the individual to God as a vessel through whom the life of God can be expressed unhindered.

The life of Christ reproduced in man is revealed here by the testimony of our Lord Jesus Christ to the people in John chapter 8:

"So, Jesus said, "When you have lifted up the Son of Man on the cross, then you will understand that I AM he. I do nothing on my own but say only what the Father taught me. And the one who sent me is with me—he has not deserted me. For I always do what pleases him."

—John 8:28-29 (NLT2)

The original intent of God in sending our Lord Jesus Christ is to be the first model and then allow the Holy Spirit to reproduce His very life in our lives as revealed here in this Scripture:

"For God knew his people in advance, and he chose them to become like his Son so that his Son would be the firstborn among many brothers and sisters.

—Romans 8:29 (NLT2)

CONVERSATIONAL PRAYER AND SPIRITUAL EMPOWERMENT

The essence of this is believing and confessing the truth of Scripture. There are confessions of faith that actualize God's power in our lives.

The first step is to believe in your heart and confess with your mouth that when our Lord and Savior Jesus Christ died on the Cross of Calvary for the sins of all humanity, your sins were included. Here is one way to pray these:

Lord Jesus, I believe with all my heart that You died for my sins. My old life of sin and rebellion against God died with You on that Cross of Calvary and was buried with You in that grave.

I believe with all my heart that when You rose from the dead, that resurrection morning, I also rose with You to a new life of holiness and obedience to God in all things.

- The second confession is an invitation:

Lord Jesus, please come into my heart and be my Lord and Savior. I confess with my mouth, what I believe in my heart, that You Jesus, are my Lord and Savior. Let the whole world hear me declare: JESUS IS MY LORD AND SAVIOUR, to the glory of God the Father in Jesus name, Amen.

- Now comes the invitation to the Holy Spirit.

O Thou Spirit of the Living God, please come and live in my heart. I give You complete liberty to express the life and power of Christ through me. I receive the grace of obedience now, so that I may follow You daily until I get to heaven, in Jesus name I pray, Amen.

BAPTISM OF THE HOLY SPIRIT

The baptism of the Holy Spirit is a promise of the Father as revealed in Acts 2:38-39 (NLT2)

"Peter replied, 'Each of you must repent of your sins, turn to God, and be baptized in the name of Jesus Christ to show that you have received forgiveness for your sins. Then you will receive the gift of the Holy Spirit. This promise is to you, and to your children, and even to the Gentiles—all who have been called by the Lord our God."

O LORD my God, may it please You to baptize me with Your Holy Spirit as You did on the day of Pentecost. I desire to be a witness of the death and resurrection of Jesus Christ and His life as the Saviour of all humanity. I confess now that I am filled with the Holy Spirit. From this moment, I will express the life and power of Christ to my world, in Jesus' name, Amen.

Printed in Great Britain
by Amazon

78259128R00081